AN INDEX OF AROUND ME

by

Gary Llama

OVOLR! / DEBACKLE
RICHMOND, VIRGINIA

As first published in the Zines:

'Five Years'
© 2011, Gary Llama, OVOLR! / DEBACKLE

'Navigating Known Terrain'
© 2012, Gary Llama, OVOLR! / DEBACKLE

'Growing Into Something'
© 2012, Gary Llama, OVOLR! / DEBACKLE

OVOLR! / DEBACKLE
RICHMOND, VA USA

to living an examined life

Forward

It's weird. Writing became a big thing for me in 2005. I was just over a period of health issues, and inspired by the writing of Howard Zinn and C. Wright Mills, I began cataloging my views on things. I shouldn't say cataloging, as much as exploring.

For years, my voice was dead. It was something I had enjoyed when younger, playing in a couple political punk bands, I had been privy to the luxury of a medium, and something of an audience. But as I moved from behind the instruments, to behind the mixing board, I found myself voiceless. And that didn't sit right with me.

So I began to write.

And with the writing came a sense of importance to sharing these thoughts. Some of the stuff here was published as zines. Other stuff was shared on my website. And still other things were not shared at all.

I've never been one much for fear of sharing, but an odd thing has happened: As I've written more, and seen more of an audience read my thoughts, I've become more resistant to sharing my thoughts. "Why bother?" I think to myself.

It isn't that I don't care, so much as I've come to view the world in a much more relative manner. And I thought my essays reflect this, the underlying model, a view of a net positive telling me 'share', has begun to be questioned. And not for no reason.

I write for the hopeful. I write for the person inside myself that needs that bit of inspiration. That needs to see the possibilities. I also write because I believe the act of sharing is one of the best things a human being can do. To connect with others through sharing experience, we find the tid-bits we can relate to, and the wall of separation crumbles a bit. It comes from a place of wanting us to be equal. Believe that.

I've also become more questioning of motivation. While sharing is a great thing, the writing has become something I feel good about, because it makes me feel good. But I become cautious of making sure a good intention is there. I feel the worst thing I could do besides not share, is write to please my ego. So I police the ego in me, probably more than I should sometimes.

I've been in a very introspective state the last year. Part of it, because the concept of 'meaning' and 'value' in my life has been eclipsed by the birth of my daughter, something to which any creative endeavor I can produce does not stand a chance of comparing to. So there is a little bit of 'Why bother?" considering I can just sit here and see her smile, and be full filled in a way I could not have imagined possible.

For a few years, I had used a little thought as a device to help me through depression. I would simply imagine that, somewhere in my future, a partner that I loved, and my child, were waiting for me to come home. Like literally, I would see a picture of these folks in my head, somewhat shadowy, but warm, the child waiting by a window, looking eagerly, for me to arrive from the rain. Like I was coming home from work.

To a person who had been single for a couple years, and divorced before that, it seemed unfathomably future-tense to think such a thing. For someone with health problems and a hard time holding steady work, it seemed even more future-tense.

But within a couple years, something I had imagined to be a 10-20 year goal, came true. The funniest part is

I didn't even realize it had come true until just a few days ago, my daughter now 7 months old.

Mind-blowing. I thought 'well that is amazing!' But then I thought, 'what will I use for my new device to get through depression?' And the problem solves itself. One look at my daughter, and the reality to the life I have ahead with her, and my spouse, exceeds anything I could hope or imagine.

When something like that, so good, so happy, comes into your life, it makes you rebuild the perspective on where you place value with other things.

And so I'm sitting here, her smiling at me, my spouse smiling at me, typing this text, in an attempt to face some fears, some uncertainty, and do what has always felt right to me, share.

Gary Llama, Jan 6 2014

FIVE YEARS

REVOLUTIONS OCCUR ONE PERSON AT A TIME:

A MANIFESTO OF REASON, RATIONALITY, AND SELF

17 September 2005
Revised July 23, 2006

Every day, ordinary people make simple, seemingly-harmless and not-so-harmless decisions that add up to the daily actions of the populace as a whole. Sometimes the results seem uneventful. Sometimes they are catastrophic. At all times they are human.

On Revolution...

Revolution occurs one person at time. There is no mass that needs to be rallied. Instead, rally the individual; Rally yourself. Live your life the way you think life should be lived. The populace is as close as the man next to you.

1. Consent
Our consent is our only true currency. Use it wisely.

2. Boogey men
There are no "boogey men" that can circumvent

consent in our society.

3. Consumerism
Buy and Sell the things you think should be bought and sold. Create the market you believe in.

4. Voting
Vote for what you believe in, not what you can rationalize.

5. Politics
Politics is the replacement of a system of rationality based on reason with a system of rationality based on calculation. Circumvent politics by countering it with reason.

6. Power stems from the barrel of power
Defending an idea with a gun only reinforces the idea of defending things with a gun.

7. War
Wars are being fought as solutions because people are willing to fight wars as solutions.

8. Masters ("us vs. them")
To hold contempt for "them" puts your contempt inevitably against yourself. There is only "us".

9. Prejudice and Racism

To dislike someone because of their difference is to dislike someone because they are human.

10. Failure
Respect the fallibility of the man next to you and you will respect your own humanity.

11. Success
Success is whatever we believe makes us successful.

12. Media
The quality of our information is the basis of the quality of our education. Report of failure as much as success.

13. Art
Art is the mechanism of discovery by which we define the extremes of our being. We must create the art we dream, rather than the art we can rationalize.

14. Business
Business is a mechanism of humanity, not its master.

THE CALORIC VALUE OF A DOLLAR:

A movement towards calculating actual consumption

11 November 2005

Overview:
Each person must expend some amount of energy to earn one dollar. The sum of energy expended may vary greatly from person to person. Therefore, the common dollar as we know it may have a greater or lesser amount of caloric dependency depending upon the channel through which it was earned.

Why this is important:
As money is one of the basic elements studied in the evaluation of sustainable economies, one must fully understand the personal caloric expenditure and it's variables in order to completely grasp the gross caloric investment in each person's dollar.

Sally
For sally to earn money she must work in a store. She drives to her work in her car. She works an average of 20 hours per week (4 hours per day), at the hourly rate of $12 per hour after taxes. During her work day she eats one meal.

Variable 1: Transportation
Sally drives an average of 20 miles to work each day in an older car that annually requires an average of $2500 in operating costs per year.

Let us suppose that $500 of those costs are gasoline, $1000 are insurance, and $1000 go to actual repair of the vehicle.

Let us then assume that the insurance requires 1000 calories of energy to be expended in its issuance, an average of 20000 calories are expended in the production off replacement car parts and repair labor annually, and that the gas requires an average of 1000 per barrel, and that sally's $500 actually purchases her 10 barrels.

For the sake of calculation let us assume these averages can be broken into an hourly cost as follow:

Category	Calories Consumed	Cost
Repair	2	$0.11
Insurance	0.10	$0.11
Gas	11	$0.05

Variable 2: Food
She requires consumption of 1800 calories on daily

average, of which 600 may be consumed and expended during actual work. Let us suppose this meal cost $5 to prepare.

The caloric production requirements of the food must be factored into her total calorie expenditure. Let us say that she eats a hamburger for lunch, French fries, a soft drink. Let us suppose that this meal ends up at a net value of 600 calories.

That would be 600 calories, right?

Well yes, but the amount of calories expended in producing the hamburger, French fries, and coke is completely overlooked, thereby giving us a false reading of the actual gross calorie expenditure she has caused to be used in her eating of the meal.

The actual amount of calories required to produce her meal will typically be much higher than the actual yield. One must factor the production of the food (feeding the cattle, growing the potatoes, producing the soft drink) and all of these actions require calories to be expended. Additionally, one must factor in the amount of energy needed to package, ship, sell, and cook (if required) the items she will eat. All of this energy has an inherent caloric value.

Let us suppose, for the sake of illustrating this model,

that the actual caloric expenditure of the meal was valued at around 2000 gross calories.

So food would add 2000 gross calories to Sally's chart. The actual amount Sally actually received from the food was 600. Leaving a caloric debt of about 1400 calories. Which averages to a per work hour cost of...

(Divide by 4 work hours)

Category	Calories Consumed	Cost
Food	500	$1.25

Variable 3: Environment
Sally works at a standalone store. For her to be able to work, the store must have electricity, running water, a phone. It must also sell products or services at some point to earn money (it's a business, after all).

Let us say in 1 hour she works, the store requires a gross 30,000 calories in utilities to be expended.

Let us also assume that she will sell 1 products in 1 hour of which each require 10,000 calories to be used to produce.

Category	Calories Consumed	Cost
Store	30,000	$0.00
Products	10,000	$0.00

Sally lives in an apartment, and while she works at the store her apartment is using a small amount of energy which must be factored in for she is paying for it while working.

Let us assume that her apartment uses 1,000 calories of energy during one hour off her work, and requires $1.36 in money for rent and utilities.

Category	Calories Consumed	Cost
Apartment	1,000	$1.36

Now we must add it all up.

Category	Calories Consumed	Cost
Transportation	13.10	$0.27
Food	500	$1.25
Environment	41,000	$1.36
Total	41,513	$2.87

That brings us to 41,513.10 calories expended to produce 1 hour of work. At $12 per hour, that averages to 3,459.425 calories expended to earn one dollar.

So, $1 = 3,459.425 calories for Sally

Of course, there was also money required to be paid for these items which required Sally's labor under these conditions. Thus we must total up the money spent, and multiply the calories per dollar sally spends against the cost.

Category	Calories Consumed	Cost
Transportation	13.10	$0.27
Food	500	$1.25
Environment	41,000	$1.36
Total	41,513	$2.87

Total cost is $2.87 per hour, bringing the total hourly cost in calories to 9,928.55

Joe

For Joe to earn money he works from home as a technical consultant. He works an average of 20 hours per week (4 hours per day), at the hourly rate of $20 per hour after taxes. During his work day he eats one meal.

Variable 1: Transportation

Joe doesn't drive to work, but he still owns a bike to get around town.

Let us suppose that Joe's bike requires $100 of maintenance per year.

Let us then assume of the $100, $60 goes to tires of

which require 12000 calories to produce. The remaining $40 goes towards maintenance labor, which requires about 400 calories to be expended. For the sake of calculation let us assume these averages can be broken into an hourly cost as follow:

Category	Calories Consumed	Cost
Tires	1.36	$0.006
Labor	0.04	$0.004
Total	1.40	$0.010

Variable 2: Food
Joe requires consumption of 2000 calories on daily average, of which 600 may be consumed and expended during actual work. Let us suppose this meal cost $5 to prepare.

Let us say that he eats a salad for lunch, tofu, and a soda. Let us suppose that this meal ends up at a net value of 500 calories, and the actual caloric expenditure of the meal was valued at around 1000 gross calories.

So food would add 1000 gross calories to Joe's chart. The actual amount Joe actually received from the food was 500, leaving a caloric debt of about 500 calories, which averages to a per work hour cost of... (Divide by 4 work hours)

Category	Calories Consumed	Cost
Food	250	$1.25

Variable 3: Environment
As Joe works from home, the work environment is his home environment.

Let us assume that his apartment uses 1,000 calories of energy and requires $1.36 in money for rent and utilities during one hour of work.

Category	Calories Consumed	Cost
Apartment	1,000	$1.36

Now we must add Joe's totals up.

Category	Calories Consumed	Cost
Transportation	1.40	$0.010
Food	250	$1.25
Environment	1,000	$1.36
Total	1,263.1	$2.36

1,263.1 calories expended to produce 1 hour of work. At $20 per hour, that averages to 63.155 calories expended to earn one dollar.

So, $1 = 63.155 calories for Joe. The total cost to Joe per hour is $2.36, so total hourly cost in calories is

149.0458.

Sustainability
At this point we must ask; whose dollar is more easily sustained?

Category	Joe Calories	Joe Cost	Sally Calories	Sally Cost
Transportation	1.40	$0.010	13.10	$0.27
Food	250	$1.25	500	$1.25
Environment	1,000	$1.36	41,000	$1.36
Sub-total	1,263.1	$2.36	41,513	$2.87

Calories expended per dollar
Joe   149.0458
Sally   9,928.55

The numbers say Joe requires less calories to be expended to make $1.

If Joe and sally were to purchase the same item, Joe would stand to be more sustainable with it then Sally would. When Joe purchases a food item, his dollar will go farther than Sally's in total calories expended due to the differences in their lifestyles.

If Joe were to start driving a car, as Sally does, he would become less sustainable. If Joe were to require the operation of a commercial building during his work, he would become less sustainable.

ON ETHICAL CONSUMERISM: PHILOSOPHY OF ETHICAL PURCHASING

17 November 2005

A couple of years ago I noticed that damn near every one of the T-shirts in my dresser was made in countries other than the one in which I live. I began noticing that many of the other products I owned, or was going to purchase, were also being manufactured abroad. This alarmed me, not for any type of nationalist sentiment, but mainly because with such strong industry in the United States, and that fact that I live in the U.S., I would have expected to find more domestically-manufactured items.

I began research into the possible causes for this phenomenon. In the course of my search I learned about the trend of outsourcing, labor laws, environmental laws, NAFTA, and every other policy and practice that encourages this sort of thing. I began to realize that the main reasons for such a shift seemed to be with lowering product cost, be it by reducing the cost of labor (paying workers less money, usually by operating in countries with poor labor regulations and enforcement) or by being able to sidestep environmental standards (by producing in countries that do not have the standards, regulations, and fines that the U.S has).

Of course, a lower cost of manufacture would generally result in an overall lower product cost, which could mean a lower selling price is possible. But I didn't remember paying any less for my t-shirts, my guitar, my shoes, my computer. In all actuality, I remembered paying a bit more than I was comfortable with. And so it would seem, while the products were being made cheaper and cheaper, the manufacturers kept right on selling as if nothing had changed. This angered me.

Intrigued, I jumped head first into learning the details of these practices; I read stories of the North Carolina garment industry being cut in half, from a strong production center to little more than corporate headquarters for the former inhabitants; I read of manufacturers (like Fender Musical Instruments Corporation, and Volkswagen AG) who setup factories in Mexico, where they are immune to EPA and U.S. labor regulations despite the U.S. being their main North American market for sale of products; I learned of many U.S. brands that now made all their products abroad. In some cases, the companies seemed in opposition to moving overseas, but sighted the lower operating costs of competition as the primary reason for their move. Some companies retained a small U.S factory, others sent everything to Asia or South America. Very few remained all U.S.-made.

At the time, I was looking for a new DVD player for my home. I began searching for a suitable product, but I also looked at the country of origin. Surely, a Sony (Japanese) DVD player would still be made in japan, or a Rotel (UK) deck made in Britain. I was shocked to find the Sony made in Malaysia, the Rotel made in china. The only ones I could find that were produced in a country with civilized labor enforcement and regulation was a DVD player by Panasonic (japan), actually still made in japan. I purchased it promptly.

My core interest in this subject snowballed. I began looking at everything I purchased, researching alternatives to the questionable, and holding off on purchasing till an alternative was found. I began compiling a mental list of the products I would be comfortable purchasing.

This all required a substantial amount of my own time, and sometimes a bit of personal sacrifice, but it all hinged on my dedication to one principle I felt I could not violate: That as a citizen of a so-called first world nation, I must use the privilege of my access to information, my access to ethical debate, the value of my money, and overall market knowledge to try and purchase things that I believe are in accordance with the way I wish the capitalist market to operate; that regardless of how many companies are doing what and where, I am responsible for the market I help to create. My dollar is a vote for a system of practices, and in a multi-national market that is ruled by corporations and substantiated by consumer consent, my dollar is my only means of exerting appreciable force towards the practices I feel comfortable with.

Regardless of consciousness on the subject, the fact is my money is going to support an idea. The idea I choose to support could be one of two things;

      1. Selective consumption, purchasing only from those who respect the worker and environment, and help to provide a more sustainable world
      2. Mass consumption at all costs, at the cost of the health and rights of workers, and/or at the cost of the longevity and preservation of environment.

I choose the first way, supporting the system I actually believe in. Many folks choose the second way, most times I suspect, without even knowing they have a choice.

Since making this decision I have learned of many

"ethical" alternatives for the market I want to create and support with my purchases. I have also found many organizations working to help find such markets. Myself, I have started a resource website (punkrocksweatshop.org) dedicated to listing production companies specifically for the band or record label looking to produce "ethical" t-shirts.

Overall, I feel much better knowing that my purchases are helping to build something, rather than to disenfranchise the workers and the environment of the very protections the citizens of the "first world" have fought so long and hard to incorporate into their everyday life.

ON PRESERVING DISSIDENCE IN SCHOOL:

The need for a union amongst progressive teachers

25 December 2005

Back in high school I had the good fortune of taking a "social studies" class that was not part of the standard curriculum. The teacher was very enthusiastic about his class, and brought in material based on his own choices.

It was through this class that I was first exposed to Michael Moore's work by his series "TV nation". Through watching these episodes in class, I learned a good deal about the consequences of business practices in our country; seeing the unemployed laborers in Flint, Michigan, and hearing their stories. For a student living in a largely broken city such as Richmond, VA, it helped to illustrate why perhaps our own city had developed as it had.

This class built a solid groundwork in making me much more aware of the workings of our world.

The real benefit of the class was evident when talking with students who were not lucky enough to have taken this particular class; their overall level of social consciousness seem to be malaise and un-informed by comparison, even at such an early level in our course.

At some point in the year, my personal interests in the material collided with my teachers, resulting in a brief exchange in the hall, away from the ears of the class. I cannot remember the exact wording, or the issue upon which our disagreement was based, but my position was of "...and why can't we also focus on this issue?" The teacher responded with a fear of losing his job should we step too much outside the realm of the "approved curriculum".

And here is our problem: This teacher was obviously trying to show us and perspective of our country that was different from what the standard curriculum would allow, yet he still had to worry about the consequences of such actions, and first and foremost in his mind was the fear of losing his job. I cannot blame him for his fear; read about the actions of teachers in similar positions around our country and you will find many who have lost their jobs on similar grounds.

The problem is obviously one of censorship in our schools. While it is not as blatant or heavy-handed as the censorship in other nations, these well-founded fears still prevent our students from being able to learn about the world from both sides of the trenches. In America, our censorship is much lower key, put forth as an unspoken rule, placing much of the burden on the individual teacher. It is not as if there was a massive government censor breathing down his neck, instead he has to worry about the potential of just a handful of students and parents complaining till the school board folds in on the issue. And the quickest way to clean up such a mess is often just to fire the teacher.

As the tactics employed to keep such curriculum sterile are so similar to the tactics used to isolate workers from achieving better pay and work conditions, I propose that the solution be similar as well: A union for social studies teachers. Such an organization could be easily formed with a Hippocratic Oath similar to the ones used by doctors in our society. The solidarity of a union would ease the tension placed on individual teachers by being singled out for their beliefs. It could also serve as a platform to organize a much more holistic view of our society.

The overall effects of such an organization could be tremendous. Such an action would work well towards establishing a deeper consciousness in our students. On a more general level, I would suspect it would allow us a chance to bring our society as a whole to a greatness not possible with such ignorance of social issues.

As free-thinkers we must realize that our biggest obstacle in proposing social change is ignorance. And while this issue may seem quite small to the average intellectual, we must remember that our schools are ironically the place where free thought stops for some pupils. We must work to ensure that if such thought ceases, it ceases informed, and if we can help it, the intriguing reality presented by an encompassing view of our society would encourage it not to cease at all.

DISCONNECTED: NO LOGO

22 March 2006

A few months ago I decided to read Naomi Klein's book, "No Logo". The areas of the book I particularly liked dealt with the recent (and by recent I mean the last 15 years) trends of corporations to cut themselves off from owning any means of production by outsourcing their manufacturing to other countries, and with it, the companies sense of responsibility for the labor conditions under which their products are produced. I thought it was a good book overall, perhaps a bit basic, but a good primer for anyone looking to learn more about the way corporations are run these days, and sweatshops in general. I found it at my public library.

However, after reading this book I was somewhat shocked to see the following response by the author when questioned by The Guardian in 2000 about the ethics of her own purchases:

"This is not a consumer issue; it's a political issue. There is a way for us to respond as citizens that is not simply as consumers. Over and over again, people's immediate response to these issues is: what do I buy? I have to immediately solve this problem through shopping. But you can like the products and not like the corporate behavior; because the corporate behavior is a political issue, and the products are just stuff. The movement is really not about being purer-than-thou and producing a recipe for being an ethical consumer. That drains a lot of political energy" - Article

I strongly disagree with this view. The reasoning put forth in this quote frustrates me on a number of levels:

  1. How is a corporation's decision to sell a product a political issue? Do we elect Nike to represent us for shoes politically? No, we tell them we like their shoes by purchasing them, which makes this very much a consumer issue. Businesses sell things because people buy them. If people don't buy things, business will try and find something they will buy. That being said, their products may indeed influence things in a political manner, but their business model is consumerism, their motive is profit, and as a result they live and die by consumer interest, not by political persuasion.

  2. The idea that one can like a product yet not like the behavior of its producer (the corporation) completely denies what a product really is; a "product" is the product of everything that was required to produce it; corporate behavior, sweatshop labor, everything required to see it from the drawing board to the consumer's hands. To see a product minus these

aspects is to look at the item in a way that is not in accordance with reality. If I were to subscribe to this line of logic, I could simply steal money from people, and just say to myself "hey look, I have money", despite the reality that I would have stolen money. This line of reasoning is the disconnect; the wall that consumers must overcome to truly understand that the product they buy is the collective sum of labor and material. To perpetuate such a disconnect is counter-productive to everything her book supposedly stands for in the first place; exposing the truth behind big business and its sweatshop products.

I firmly believe that "Free Markets" are not built upon politics, they are built upon purchasing. And as such "Free markets" will not be changed by politics, they will be changed by ethical consumption. One can simply look to the drug war to observe how well industries that are driven by consumer demand can be eradicated by political pressure.

ON WEALTH

22 March 2006

I make no secret that I despise consumerism. However, it is not because I despise capitalism or the idea of purchasing goods, but rather, I despise the cycle of consumerism and its ability to destroy wealth in people.

The first reaction may be to think of wealth monetarily in terms of donation, and other money-related activities. But I am of the belief that money has very little to do with actual wealth. Money comes and goes in even the richest of people. Personal wealth is built in to a person's character. Their day to day life leaves them with a certain surplus of a trait or skill that they can give back to humanity. That is true wealth.

Wealth I define as "having something to give". "Something" could be anything of value, including money, but also including time, creativity, love, and other intangible things. I believe this definition of "wealth" is the wealth which we are all searching for, but we commonly accept the money-based definition to fulfill it. Perhaps because money is more easily obtained than the intangibles of love, creativity, and time.

Money can easily be obtained in a capitalist society, all one has to do is trade their time and work to obtain money. How does one obtain love, or creativity?

The capitalist system offers no simple prescription for the attainment of these things. Accordingly, money appears to be worth less than love and creativity, as these are much rarer.

One starts out in a consumer world looking to advance one's self from a position of poverty. I believe poverty is the driving force behind consumerism, and that it is the default state of consumerism as well.

People obtain in consumerism to have "more", and thus to be farther from poverty. But "more" is a subjective term. One can never truly obtain "more". Because the whole idea of "more" is "more than". You can never have more than you actually have, can you? And so the consumer always eventually comes back to feeling like "more" would be better, and that staying at the current position of attainment is staying closer to poverty.

Poverty could be summed up as "having less than". As such, I believe poverty continuously stays a threat through consumerism because our actual definition of poverty in this country seems to rely on "less", which has the ambiguity of "more", and never considers balance. It only says "less than you currently have". Thus we are posed with a choice when deciding whether to engage in consumerism, do we want to have more, or less? The psychological impact of such a question will indubitably almost always end with the same response.

I believe poverty has little to do with lack of money. My goal is wealth in one's soul. I believe true wealth can be ascertained by answering one simple question: Do you have something to give to the world?

PUBLIC BOOKS; OR, WHY I LIKE THE LIBRARY

22 March 2006

There is something depressing about bookstores: Thousands of different books, multiple copies of each, held captive in the stagnant din of a commercial space for $18-$25 apiece. It's not that I don't want to read the books, I do. I just don't want to own them. Can you really own a book? You can own a copy, but at the end of the day you must pay for its space in your home. You must provide shelf space for it to live. And in reality, most books I read once, and never again.

The library is an inspiring place. Perhaps because it's model of providing the book is very much like the model of how I will use its information: I do not own the information learned from reading a book, I borrow the information. The work itself belongs to the author. And though I may reference and build from the ideas presented in a book, but I will never own the idea.

The intellectual's bookshelf also bothers me: It serves almost as a degree in of itself; A declaration of worthiness for the individual. A vain attempt to align oneself with the creative practices of other men through material association. "Look at all these books I have read", they say. But it serves no other practical purpose. For the working intellectual, referencing could be done as easy via a list of books in a public library as in a private library. And that is the whole point; I detest private libraries, I suppose, because I detest the idea of private information. The majority of the books I read are the product of a large collection of research by an author. Compiling it doesn't mean the author owns the information provided. It simply means he owns the position he arrived at; the product of assembly and personal skew, as one may own the rights to a sound recording, while not actually owning the rights to the music.

I think we must ask ourselves; to what is the purpose of information? I would say it is to inform. But if a book has been read by a person, what benefit does it serve collecting dust in a private library?

Public Libraries excite me, as they are a source of information available to any man, women, or child at the price of simply providing a picture ID. They are an efficient use of resources; one book, many people. A book from a public library is a story in itself: The worn binding, pages of interest dog-eared and highlighted. It's comforting to open a used book, the binding broken in already. Opening a new book can seem violent, the spine cracking and resisting.

Of course, this perspective doesn't bode well for authors looking to make money from their writing. But I really don't care. Does capitalism always have to be the motivating factor behind research? Writing? Art?

PURCHASE EVALUATION:

A formula to aid in calculating compatibility with purchases.

28 August 2007

So I've made a small list of questions to run by myself when contemplating obtaining anything, to help me decide if something is compatible with my way of life and beliefs. It was designed for clothing, but it can be applied to anything by modifying each variable to the closest likewise quality.

1. Do I like the fit?
2. Do I like the function?
3. Is it free of trends?
4. Will it last?
5. a) is it ethical? b) Is there an ethical alternative?

These are answered yes or no, then the "yes's are counted and tallied against the number of questions.

- 4 out of 5 and above are a safe bet.
- 3 deserves suspicion.
- 2 and lower are not compatible with me.

Criteria Overview
A brief overview of the choices of questions and why.
Do I like the fit?

- Does design work towards the goal of the item, does it hinder operation? Do I like the aesthetics?

Do I like the function?
- Does the item do what I need it to do? Do I like how it accomplishes its function?

Is it free from Trends?
- Does the item have a true use, or is it here for reasons of trivial consumption? Generally, the trendiness of an item may impair future supply of replacement parts, or make you just want to get rid of it prematurely.

Will it last?
- Is its expected longevity good for the purposes you wish to employ it? The sustainability could also be factored here.

Is it Ethical?
- Does it exist in accordance with your ethics?
The question regarding ethics is in two parts. Answer B is recursive and dominate over the first. A "yes" on part "a" requires no further answer from "b". A "no" on "a" with a yes on "b", changes the full answer to a "no". A "no-no" changes the answer to a "yes".

The system is designed to rate an item in accordance with your perception of it. However, you must know some information about the item to accurately calculate it. And of course, over time its rating may change as more information on the item becomes available. Basically, it's a formula that I have used for a long time, but never articulated into a set number of steps or process until now.

Example
An example of how to use it would be:

Widget
1. y
2. y
3. n
4. y
5. y (a. n, b. n)
Total: 4/5

Now I'm just running through everything I can think of and seeing how the answers stack up.

PROCESS VERSUS PRODUCT

21 April 2008

The work of science and art are of process. Not to be confused with product. Others will assemble our work, if relevant. Our purpose is to produce process. We will not be remembered. We will not be celebrated. And will be very sparsely rewarded if at all. Our reward must be the process. And so we must focus on what excites us.

NON-PLACE AND THE RATIONALIZATION OF LIFE

25 April 2008

Thesis Statement: In a world dominated by the homogenized place, the non-place offers a space to escape the rationalization of everyday life.

The Condemnation of Place

The average American may now find his life somewhat alienating. He lives in a community segregated by income and resulting class, works in a building built as some modernist derivation of a rectangle, and spends much of his time traversing between the two in his car, alone. Wherever he finds himself, he seems to be out of scale with the world around him, a world designed to be traveled via car. And so he submits to a dependence on his automobile along with other means of mechanization to navigate the avenues of his life (Kunstler, 1993).

Such is the difficulty of the modern American. And in an attempt to justify the wait, the dependence on externalities, he must rationalize his actions and his way of life. The difficulty begins when the material to be rationalized, is not rational in occurrence with reasoning he accepts.

This presents a proverbial House-of-Cards effect on the self. If he was to identify the rational which reasoning he does not accept, he may begin to unravel the fabric of his livelihood, his work and domestic life, and the foundations he has built his life upon. It is really not a question of "would", for most of us would find that the majority of our rational is an effect of agreement based on survival rather than actual agreement based on understood reasoning. The question is rather: Will he find enough time between the mechanization of his rational world, to find the first thread to pull?

The Non-Place

If there were a space where Man can unravel the fabric of his rationalization, it would be in a place free from the mechanisms that bind him to his accepted reality. This is a similar thought to the rationalization of drug use in 1960s counterculture. But where the counterculture sought to limit the restrictions of their milieu by means of elevated dopamine levels, an alternative approach relies on limiting the contextual implications of place, by entering into the ether of the physical realm.

Such a place would be a non-place, as described by Marc Auge:

"If a place can be defined as relational, historical and concerned with identity, then a place which cannot be defined as relational, or historical, or concerned with identity will be a non-place." (Auge p 77)

Further:

" Place and non-place are rather like opposite polarities: the first is never completely erased, the second never totally completed" But non-places are the real measure of our time - by totaling all the air, rail, and motorway routes, the mobile cabins called "means of transport" (aircraft, trains, and road vehicles), the airports and railway stations, hotel chains, leisure parks, large retail outlets, and finally the complex skein of cable and wireless networks that mobilize extraterrestrial space for the purposes of communication" (Auge p 79)

But where the rest of the description put forth in Auge's work condemns the non-place for what they loose of an individual's identity, I came to see the beauty of these spaces in relation to the entrapments of the modern place.

In talking to a friend about the subject of this paper, He stated that it was precisely the non-place that allowed him to reconnect with himself (and, I assume, his identity): the quiet car ride, waiting in the airport lounge area; it was these spaces where he felt disconnected from the exterior world in such a way that it facilitated connection with his inner-self, more-so than he felt possible in a place.

There are similarities between the non-place and the place: Both reek of homogeneity; both may be particularly bland in an aesthetic sense. In the modern suburb we find many objects that serve as a nod to historical reference, such as the styles of home architecture. In his book, Geography of Nowhere, James Kunstler places much of the blame for the perceived "placeless-ness" of the suburb on historical references by architecture implemented in cheap method to give the home an appearance of historical significance, such as the Georgian-style of southern homes to the Greco-Roman style (Kunstler, p150). In such cases, we assign these architectural elements a symbolic agency, a representational meaning (Smith, p 132). Now meaningful, we rationalize these occurrences under a judgment of aesthetics, and in the process rationalize their faux connections into our lives.

The non-place lacks such pretension in the sense that we do not assign its elements any agency. We deem their elements to not be "functionally important", and in the process assign them no agency with reference to symbolism (Smith, p 144). In short, we demand the places where we build our lives to have authentic historical, geographical, and identity elements, but we demand none of these from the non-place.

Utilizing the non-place as a space to foster connection with our self would be to appropriate these spaces in the way the Situationist's utilized irregular city layouts to encourage drift; crossing space as a means to engage in situations of emotional significance (Sadler, 1998).

The Paradox of the Non-place

While it may seem as though the environment of a non-place would have to be serene to foster such connections, the environment is typically anything but. In the cases of waiting areas for transportation, the volume of people in the vicinity may be overwhelming, and the levels of sound from passing vehicles deafening. The levels of visual noise, most notably in the form of commercial advertising, may be completely saturated. And personal privacy is at a significantly lower level than one would find in their home. Yet here, submitted to the conformity of the space, we find a sense of freedom. Perhaps a freedom to be uniform. Such thought does not bode well for the American concept of freedom as an extremely individualized and almost decadent behavior. Auge finds here, we submit to the mechanization of conformity:

A person entering the space of non-place is relieved of his determinants. He becomes no more than what he does or experiences in the role of passenger, customer, or driver; he *tastes for a while; the passives joys of identity loss, and the more active pleasure of role-playing' the passenger through non-places retrieves his identity only t Customs, at the tollbooth, at the checkout counte*r" (Auge, p 103)

So we find ourselves lost in the milieu of the non-place but in a significantly intrusive environment. I suspect if the same conditions existed in the home, the place, he might object and refuse to go along accordingly. The paradox is, in essence, that in addition to assigning its elements no agency in symbolism, in the non-place we also assume no ownership (control) for the conditions of our surroundings. Finding ourselves powerless to change or be held responsible for them, we submit to their existence.

Extending the definition of the non-place
The physical definition of a non-place is very broad, and I suspect many avenues of escapism or fantasy might be qualified as the non-place, some not being physical places at all: digital networks, telephone calls, text messaging. All of these things provide a framework of rules (implied as boundaries, just as the physical place provides walls), and allow for a transaction to occur, a dialog, for some form of business to occur in, and in a sense establish a loose place for the exchange. While we may not think of the landscape of a telephone call or text message, we have imagined the

landscape of the Internet. The radio and the pop-songs it plays may also continue on this pattern, establishing a base of rules (musical repetition, rhythm and tempo) and facilitate a transaction (receiving the music, lyrics). For all of these, there is a sense of leaving in the cessation of the task. And in this sense, they have created a place, and in its lack of definition, a non-place.

Conclusion

Through a loss of identity, or temporary lack of reference to symbolism, the non-place provides a place to escape the agency of place. Through observation of the non-place, we can realize the constrictions of place. We also see a shift in what we deem acceptable in terms of aesthetics of environment. Additionally, we may see elements of non-place in any space were we conduct a transaction by a set of rules.

However, one must wonder about implications of the non-place on society. While short-term identity loss may be fine for a passenger, I am interested in the long-term effects on daily life. Relief may begin to parallel fantasy. Digital environments may provide a space where both place and non-place exist simultaneously, sometimes within the same domain of each other, where the definitions of history, identity, and geography are blurred by the relativism inherent in a digital system. Are the virtual worlds of Second Life, or of a video game, a non-place? And further, are the actions taken within a non-place, a truer action of actor than those taken in a place, with relevance to what we desire? And is the difference due to dissociation with identity, or rather, a lack of symbolic agency imposed by the place? As we merge our lives with the virtual landscape of digital technologies, it is these questions we must answer.

Reference:

Auge, Marc. Non-places: introduction to an anthropology of super modernity. London: Verso, 1995.

Kunstler, James Howard. The Geography of Nowhere: the rise and decline of America's man-made landscape. New York: Simon & Schuster, 1993.

Sadler, Simon. The Situationalist City. Cambridge: The MIT Press, 1998.

Smith, Ronald W. Bugni, Valerie. Symbolic Interaction Theory and Architecture. Symbolic Interaction , Vol. 29, Issue 2, pp. 123–155

MEDIATING THE SELF
THROUGH THE WEB

21 April 2008

I have been wondering over the past few months about the connection between a media-saturated society, reality, and the sudden burst of user-generated media content on the internet. I have begun to form a theory, mainly, that user generated content is a way for a person to authenticate themselves by encoding elements of their lives into media formats that are relied upon for the transmission of important events of reality.

The basic thought is this: we receive information about the world around us through various forms of media. As we become accustomed to receiving this information in these formats, about people, places, and things which we deem important, we begin to associate worthiness with the media format itself. And so, we attempt to make our lives seem more 'real' relative to our mediated surroundings; essentially, by mediating our own lives via these formats.

We also begin to associate the unintentional characteristics inherent in each format with importance. With each media format comes an artifact; something that is placed on the message being transmitted unintentionally; the grain of film, the half-tone print of a newspaper photo, and the hiss of analog tape. As we receive information that we value as important through these media, we begin to associate the artifacts inherent in the media with the importance of the message as well. Consequently, we may develop an emotional response/attraction to these artifacts. From my days of being an audio recording engineer, I can remember countless arguments of analog tape vs. digital recordings centered around the "magical" (read: emotional attachment) qualities of tape vs. the lifeless quality of digital. While technically, digital recording has its artifacts, we were not accustomed to them, and most importantly, the format artifacts were unlike the artifacts of analog of which we had spent years developing an attachment to. I've heard the same romanticism about film grain in analog vs. digital photography, and I'm sure it goes on and on, through many fields and many technologies.

Specifically, I've wondered about this phenomenon with regards to the photo sharing site, Flickr. On the site, one can view a large amount of photography; from beautiful images from photo amateurs and professionals to vernacular everyday items; people's pets, the contents of their book bags. My theory is that by photographing these items they become validated to an audience who has become accustomed to seeing important information represented in the context of media, in this case the photograph, with all of its inherent artifacts; extreme color saturations (or lack of), the crop of the image itself, etc.

This theory extends the ideas of representation of self through material popularized by Erving Goffman, assigning agency to material, etc., but updated for the new situations presented by the web. It also follows form of the research I have read on Symbolic Interaction within the realm of architecture. The following sources may provide further insight:

Reference

Riggins, Stephen Harold. The power of things: The role of domestic objects in the presentation of self. Beyond Goffman. Berlin: Mouton de Gruyter. 1990

Smith, Ronald W. Bugni, Valerie. Symbolic Interaction Theory and Architecture. Symbolic Interaction , Vol. 29, Issue 2, pp. 123–155

FINDING THE POINT OF DECLINING UTILITY

17 September 2008

I know I take things for granted. It seems like an inevitability of exposure: the more you experience a thing, the less you appreciate it. The trick seems to be identifying the point at which you begin to not appreciate a thing anymore, and staying there. Past this point, it can be said something has a declining utility.

Finding that point has been a personal project of mine for the last few years. I do it with everything: food, drink, smoking, clothing, entertainment. With static things, it's rather easy to control intake. But with dynamic things, like relationships with other human beings, it is much more difficult.

The goal is two-fold: 1) mindfulness of overall consumption, and 2) efficiency. The engineer in me loves this because essentially I am engineering my life for more efficiency. The eco-conscious part of me loves it because I am reducing my waste, and overall footprint on society. It's something I enjoy spending time thinking about.

However, like life itself, this is an exploratory process. Some things will make sense on paper, yet may not gel with the things you want from your life. I find it extremely important to not beat yourself up about things like this, and to take a soft-handed approach. Hard rules have a declining utility of their own.

YOUTUBE AS PROCESS

20 October 2008

This was originally posted on my school blog as part of a class exploring Learning with Digital Media

Over the past couple years, I have been on a quest to understand aesthetics. My jump off point was branding, (why do we respond to branding) and then exploring emotional connections to experience and its connection to consumerism. I came across an important realization in this: given two items, people will react stronger to the one they have established an emotional connection to. Branding, in a sense, is the practice of generating that story in a top-down manner, from the producer out. We see commercials telling us the stories we could be telling others, if only we are to buy this product. Sometimes the story is a community, a top-down imitation of social connection: Join our club. Mac User, jeep driver. We then distill these stories and assign them agency, emulating their desired goal and in a sense, giving them authenticity. After a while, I began to see certain logos representing something of a granfalloon, a concept I give much weight to.

In the process of exploring this, I did what only seemed natural: I used my life as a model, and explored my own connection with branding and brands. I explored the stories I told myself of things, and questioned whether they were created by me, or someone else. I began to feel strongly that I would not let myself do anything to perpetuate branding myth, and in turn, began to actively seek ways to destroy their aesthetic power.

Such a process does not simply end here though, and one will find themselves unravelling anything that may exist as rationalized to divulge reasoning. It's blown my ability to do any graphic design pretty much to hell.

Tonight, while watching an anthropological introduction to YouTube, I came to see a connection between the issues explored and some of these thoughts on aesthetics. For one: most youtubers look goofy. While some folks dedicate their lives to calling out those who violate the social norms, I tend to embrace anything that might appear goofy, for its presence may signal something truly worthwhile, authenticity. This process reminds me of a concept Stephan Sagmeister has put forth in recent work "trying to look good limits my life". While playing social policeman, we tend to put more value on the aesthetic, the product, what is visible, than to the process, the feeling, and that is where we make life.

And YouTube seems to have no pretense of product. Gone are the aesthetic rules which predominate contemporary film and art, YouTube is about process. Yet there is more connection going on there than all the modern art of today can pretend to allude to. Human beings, riffing off of one another, to create things.

Against a landscape of emotional prescription, YouTube is a truffle.

And like anything remotely authentic, there is a team of marketing folks determined to work that fertile field to a capital advantage. As a by-product, they turn the aesthetic into cliché, essentially strip mining culture until even the most unnerved is too self-aware to continue posting with any dignity, feeling aped out of their own method. And then they move on.

And they have been moving on. What we see on YouTube is not the beginning of something, or the end. It's a continuation of people making media work for them, as they have been doing for many decades. Early in the pamphleteers, on to zine culture, community access shows, punk rock, electronic music scenes, etc. All providing an outlet of unscripted catharsis up until the point that emulation by corporateers makes the channel become cliché, fraudulent, suspicious, and faddish.

CREATING THE ART EXPERIENCE

27 October 2008

A lull in art production.
I like the definition of art as anything that gives the viewer an "art experience". In other words, it's more than a pleasing image.

I feel a lot of the art I have created simply references a symbology or technique, so that it looks like art. My current path is to create things that facilitate the art experience with as little syntax attached, as is possible.

So, if I succeed in making an experience for you, you may just say "that's interesting", but not even think of it as art. That is what I am aiming for.

As you may gather, I'm in an exploratory state with this right now. And somewhere along the line, I erased my archive of past works. I'm taking it as a new beginning. I have spent much of my recent time observing the creation process of others, offering occasional input, but listening more than speaking.

I hope to begin creating some interesting things soon.

CALCULATING VALUE

02 January 2009

One of the difficulties in exploring new things in life, be it an activity or tool/technology, is assessing the value, or the benefit it brings to me. Sometimes I may miss the actual value something provides by paying attention more to aesthetic or philosophical attributes of a thing, rather than what it actually does for me.

To counteract this, I came up with this little equation.
Reward ÷ Time = Value

To use: Take the thing you want to assess, and rank it's variables of Reward received and Time invested, then calculate.

Example:

	Tool A	Tool B
Reward	4	8
Time	6	3
Value	0.6	2.6

In this situation Tool B has more Value (Reward Ã• Time = Value) than Tool A.

OPEN STANDARDS AND THE PUBLIC GOOD

03 January 2009

The USPS, Fed Ex, and UPS all maintain their own distribution networks. Intel, AMD, IBM, and Motorola all develop separate microchip architectures. Virtually every automaker is currently developing alternative fuel engines to varying degrees of success. And each is closed off from the other, as if they existed in a different world.

I can't help but wonder: How much farther ahead would technology be if developers spent their time creating and refining new functionality, instead of replicating existing systems?

Imagine if developers worked together, releasing their work as open technologies, standards upon which others could build new functionality. Think of the possibilities: Drug companies working on vaccines, starting with the best available work. Hybrid and alternative engine development, tuning the best available systems. Essentially, a world where developers start from the best of what other developers already have to offer. All energy being spent innovating, rather than recreating.

We live in a world where much effort is wasted in redundancy. We replicate functionality in the name of patentable proprietary systems. And to what benefit? For the public to be able to choose from a multitude of devices that accomplish the same function? The current model of development has been for private profit, with a patent and copyright system working to protect it, rooted in a belief that proprietary systems afford some benefit to the public. But what benefit is there to a public in a proprietary cure for disease, when the development model quarantines implementation and further progress to the intelligence and business plan of a single organization? It seems the majority of the benefit is for those that own the patent. And in my eyes, that profit is at the expense of the Public Good.

The world has changed since the establishment of the business practices common today. Technology affords us the ability to collaborate easily, and Open Source models exist that allow for developers to contribute collaboratively. Perhaps it's time for us to adjust our mindset of production to the way the world can work today, rather than one based on the limitations of yesterday.

Navigating Known Terrain

FULL-SPECTRUM IDEOLOGY: AS A TERMINAL CONDITION.

Throughout history, every world-view changing discovery of the sciences, has required the effected science to dismantle itself, and rebuild upon the new found tenants of the discovery. This has been met with periods of denial before acceptance by scientific communities, world-wide backlashes on the basis of conflicting ideologies, and most usually, the attempted (and sometimes succeeded) destruction of the Human Being who made the discovery.

Science is a realm that only knows what it can measure. In the cases of discoveries of whole new phenomenon, its acceptance generally depends on the ability of the old tools of measurement, to coincidentally, be able to measure the new discovery. In some cases, this is possible and new discoveries are absorbed more quickly. In other cases, heresy is declared. Essentially, scientist are tied to their tools, tools which are based on the discoveries of yesterday, to try and make sense of the discoveries of today. This causes science to be at one conservative, and the dreamers of science to be bound to the title of Heretic.

In Ideology, we see much of the same to occur. No

single Ideology will encompass the vast differences in conditions amongst the situations of the entire world. In some cases, rigid adherence to ideology as law, may permit situations justified by ideology, to occur, though their outcome may be, and may visibly be, be nothing close to the outcome or mechanism intended by the ideology.

In short, Ideologies are the scientific laws of idealists of the past.

If your goal is to introduce a new ethic, being tied to the tools of the old may make such work counterproductive.

Instead of accepting ideologies as an immersive religion, we should instead take them as what they are, belief systems based on the historical tendency of what has happened before, and instead adopt specific ethics, or models of operation, lightly, with a knowledge that each one's truth, is rooted in a historical situation of the past.

Deciding the efforts of today and asserting their ethical value based on an ideology rooted in the events and mechanisms of the past, is, to paraphrase Marshall McLuhan, much like driving into the future, while looking only at one's rear view mirror: You are going to run over anything new on the road ahead.

ROMANTICISING WORK: A CHRISTIAN ETHIC FOR NON-CHRISTIAN PEOPLE.

Many activists use Hard Work, as a marker of their worth. While there may be some utilitarian value to the amount of work one does for their cause, we must be cautious to not be replicating the value of hard work as a moral code

.

The Protestant Ethic, as coined and detailed by the German sociologist Max Weber in his "The Protestant Ethic and the Spirit of Capitalism, states, essentially, that to a Calvinist, one's hard work is a visible sign, and somewhat necessary, for one's salvation.

Though hard work may lead, in the case of those working on social justice issues, to a better world for Human Beings, we must realize that, assuming one does not believe in an afterlife, no bonus points will be assigned to us by any external entity as the result of working ourselves to death. The only entity that can credit us for doing this, is ourselves, and only if we believe such rigid action is inherently a good thing.

And upon further inspection, one may find that many

of the conceptions of individual autonomy, and the positive value placed on such concepts, owe much of their credence as "good" to the indoctrination of Calvinist religious thought so prevalent in Western Civilization.

Feeding the monolith: Falling in love with the group

With every position we hold, whether in a formal institution, or among grassroots movements, we run the danger of working more to protect our position, rather than to advance our end goal.

Protecting our position becomes an issue when our position becomes a part of our identity. Our position may be that of participant in a group, or leader of the group itself. Both can be absorbed into effecting how we perceive ourselves. And once absorbed into our identity, we become motivated to perpetuate the group, as we see it as a part of ourselves.

Instinctively, humans tend to build a sense of identity from the sum of their actions, and there seems to be no way to prevent this, and preventing it may be a bad idea in itself, as we all need to feel reward for our work. The trick is, to allow one's self to feel good about their work, to recognize their work as a good thing, but not feel as though they are terminally attached to any group, or position. After all, any group or job is nothing more than apparatus for effecting some end outcome, and the outcome should be the goal, not the perpetuation of the mechanism that allows us to get there.

LOST IN THE MOVEMENT: ACTIVISM AS IDENTITY

With any group, we tend to build friends, communities, and enemies the more we interact. When these elements are based off the idea of an ethic, it allows us to feel empathy and have compassion for a community in which we identify with. But we must be careful not to extract our identity from such groups. And this can seem impossibly hard to do, but it isn't really so hard.

Keeping an eye on the long term, we can appreciate the work and comradery of those around us, in a healthy way, without letting the larger group or actions define us.

There is no good way to build identity. In fact, the idea of identity tends to be corrosive, at least in the way it is applied in modern times.

Instead of looking to define the small slivers of who you are as parts of building identity, it is better just to accept yourself as a human being, and validate yourself as such. Then you will never find yourself degrading another human being for lacking the miniscule distinctions of Identity that you have extracted upon yourself. Additionally, you will be free to grow, without worry of unravelling your identity in the process.

You are a human being. You are part of an ecosystem. Your value is the same as everything around you. Be happy.

A new language: Respecting new context

As promoters of an ethic, function, or idea, we have to create a new language for our work.

Some ideas require rethinking the ways of past, fundamental flaws in ethic, and in society. In such cases, we must take care not to perpetuate the solutions of old in our language, be it visual, auditory, or written. To prevent such replication, we must become literate to the language of the old mechanisms. Too many times, I've seen new ideas put forth draped in the language of the old. The old graphic, with its inherent drive towards a conflicting solution. Revolutionary words, cloaked in a paragraph filled with words coined by the assumptions of old.

To counter this, we must become aware of Aesthetic. And work to make sure the things we present to the world, are not hobbled by the dull or conflicting work of conclusions past.

CARRIER OF THE TORCH: ACTIVISM IN CULTURE.

While activism as lifestylism may be derogatory to our specific goals and purposes, the implementation of activism in culture is a dire necessity.

Culture is the carrier of ideas. It is a trans-generational, non-stop, freight train that brings the work of those before us to the present, and allows us to know the lessons of the past, while we work on forming the ideas of the future. It allows us to stand on the shoulders of giants, per se.

All of us will die. Almost all of our work will be forgotten. All that will be remembered, is that which makes it onto the culture train.

Therefore, it is our duty, as progressors of an ethic, to leave some artifact of our work. While actions relayed to the public via experience may be curated by historians, local or worldwide, leaving such things to curators allows interpretation to be romanticized, or degraded, based on recollection of the event against the activities of the future.

And so, we must produce lasting artifacts to tie in the

historical context of what happened, with the intended meaning of our work. We must document our failures so much as our successes. Failing to do so forces the activists of tomorrow to repeat the actions of the past.

And while digital documents are easy to produce, their existence usually depends on the survival of one or two curators, especially in the model of the World Wide Web, where one entity holds responsibility for the publishing of one work, to the entire world, in a view-only, non-physically replicating model.

My advice is to encapsulate these times in song. Music is a viral language. And in zines, books, pamphlets, whatever methods can be physically produced, and then distributed to other people. We then, carrying such materials, will march on into the future, with a description of our past, in hand.

- Good Luck

Growing Into Something

BECOMING ETHICAL

With each point in life, we find ourselves in situations, of which the ethics we may or may not agree with. Our ability in these situations, to do what is in accordance with our ethics, is a matter of confidence in our ability to be ethical. If we are already ethically compromised, we may feel less able to continue without compromise.

For those who have compromised their ethics, the trick is to overcome our past compromises. Those who have been acting ethically have a distinct advantage when faced with compromise, in that their life is already good because of not-compromising, and so being ethical seems easy to obtain. On the other hand. The compromised individual may see the entire (or some part of the) good of their life as a result of some compromises. Or, they may feel that their life is already bad, so more compromises will not matter. One may even feel that by acting ethical now, they are being a hypocrite when compared to their past self, that if they act ethically now, they are essentially calling their previous compromises as unethical, or bad, and admitting this makes them feel worse about themselves.

But being ethical requires diligence to the current

situation. Remember that we always have the power to decide what we feel right to do, NOW. We are only tied to our past in the mind. Our current actions are the only way we in which we should judge ourselves in the present. Letting go of that baggage, can allow us to be who we want to be, rather than perpetuating who we have already been.

And if we are struck by an enlightenment that renders our previous actions in a negative or selfish light, we must be comfortable with the fact that as Humans, we are fallible. Learning is about being wrong, willing to risk being wrong, and willing to admit being wrong. Becoming better Human Beings is what we do with the knowledge learned.

OVERCOMING OUR OWN TRUTH

When we start looking at the world as a place where our independent actions contribute to, or diminish from, the lives of the people we live amongst, it becomes hard to go on living with our personal goals as our only guiding principle. When we see the world as interconnected and dependent upon the work of all the people in it, we begin to realize that life is not our personal playground. That we cannot be solitary. That our personal lives are dependent upon the actions of a public. The garbage man to remove our trash. The water utility to provide us water. The clerk at the grocery store to ring up our food. The baker to bake our bread. And the farmer to grow the ingredients.

And at each of these intersections of people and work, we see a disparity of income amongst the various people who make this place work. We see a disparity in the ability of some folks to keep healthy the way we do. We see a disparity in the ability of some to think they have a future they can count on. Yet we stand on the work of these individuals to pursue our own lives. We depend on their contributions as the foundation on which we build our future.

Some societies recognize this. They recognize the disparities inherent in trade. And they recognize the peculiarities of capital; that money comes most easy to those who already have it. Some folks believe that one's station in life is tied to ability. I have found these people tend to be the ones that were in abundance of ability.

So folks believe it is easy to come into money. I have found these folks to be the ones that were in the abundance of money.

And some folks believe that no matter what they do, they will always be poor. These poor folks are the ones that have grown up in an abundance of poverty.

But all of these views are nothing more than a mindset. Some may be realistic, others may be somewhat imaginary. But all of them seem as real to their envision-er as the realest thing they have ever experienced. And that's precisely why, because they have experienced it.

But not all of us experience the same things. When we look out the window to take a look at our city, we color it with our own experience; A world of ability. A world of easy money. A world of hard poverty. So when we ask ourselves what it is we want from life, we should take into account the whole picture. The farmer, the garbage man, the utility worker, the clerk. And we should imagine our own goals set up in a situation that is in accordance with this reality; that everything we do, we do with the work of others as our foundation. This is the way the world works. It would be good to recognize it. And perhaps, if we plan our own future accordingly, we will make a much richer world; for all of those working towards it.

AN APOLOGY FOR MY GENERATION

In regards to a statement made about the mythical "they" deadening society...

"They" didn't do that, my generation did.

My generation wanted to make some fucking money, just like the generation before us. But instead of being "lame" and buttoned up like our parents, whose generation never really did shit outside of become hippies, make cocaine popular in the 80's, and focus on their own selves; we decided to induce reality into TV. Maybe it was one too many diluted "after school specials" we watched. Or maybe it was our own indifference to the world, as we watched our parents bathe in the malaise of 70's, 80's and 90's comfort, and the deadening of mass culture in the name of "nice things".

So my generation decided to try and eek out a living. Mostly appropriating the things they missed from childhood, because we are basically grown up babies, craving nostalgia for things that were not that good in the first place. And with this idea, that we could change things from the inside, we went to work, and shortly became obsessed with owning the real-life versions of all the cars we drove in video games, replicating the great times of our teenage years in aesthetic, and engaging in culture as a consumeristic, after-work activity.

And somewhere in there, we created a new demographic: The mid-twenties to thirties "youth" market. We treated our young adulthood as just young, which wasn't bad in itself, but basically created yet another dumbed down, anti-intellectual demographic, alienated to real discourse, getting our news from The Daily Show, and straight-up given-up on mainstream society. Yet many of us got jobs there. But hey, "we aren't like the real mainstream, we wear t-shirts to work, and have a ping pong table, and Nerf wars!"

So basically, my generation sold your generation out, for a hot-rodded Subaru, a snowboard, conspiracy theories mistaken for intellectualism, and a perpetual sex pistols reunion, all the while putting their brains to work for the same motherfuckers that have owned everything, for always.

Sorry.

CONTROL, GOALS, AND STATUS: HOW ILLNESS TAUGHT ME TO BUILD A LIFE WHILE RESPECTING MYSELF

I opened my own business, an audio mastering studio, when I was 23.

Mastering, for those curious, is the final process before a recording is shipped out to be replicated in its end format. The final level adjustments are made in the mastering process. The goal is to make the recording sound great, everywhere, on all playback systems. The sequence of the songs is also done here, the timing of each track, fade in and fade out: taking a bunch of songs and putting them into the perfect order for the album. Essentially, mastering is where recordings turn into records, they sound like a 'record', and they feel like a 'record'. And it is done by manipulating the audio into the perfect form for what the artists wants.

So I was 23, 'mastering' audio.
I cannot stress how pretentious that should sound.

Here I was, with around two years of professional experience recording audio, 'fixing' audio recorded by people with way more experience than me. Was it absurd? A little. Was I good at it? I was decent. I remember one client remarking to a fellow engineer, early into our mastering session, that I was something of a 'prima donna', I mean here I was 23, and telling this older gentleman what was wrong with his song's audio. But I did it. I'd win over the clients because my work was good, and I'd work diligently to learn how to be better because I fell in love with the craft. Being in a supportive environment that encouraged me to try it helped as well. The studio I would freelance at as a recording engineer offered me space to setup my own room, incidentally, the old room of an engineer whom I looked up to greatly. All in all, it worked out really well. I learned the room and the equipment. I learned about business. And I began to earn clients whom respected my work as an audio engineer. And that respect, that feeling of usefulness, is why I am writing here today.

A few weeks ago, my therapist and I began talking about loss. I made a map of the loss I have had in my life, and we reflected upon it. The next week, I graphed gain. And a peculiar thing appeared: While being very honest with myself, I ranked the experience of receiving professional respect in being an audio mastering engineer, as the high point of my graph of gain. What makes this odd, is that within 2 years of opening the mastering studio, I had decided to close it down.

Around a year into running the mastering studio, my health began to get bad. Real bad. I lost about 25 pounds. For an already skinny kid, that was a huge loss. That put my weight down around 108, which as my doctor liked to call it, was 'the weight we admit folks to the hospital at'. And he did. My appetite was horribly non-existent. I felt sick whenever I ate. We tried a few different things, different diets, nothing worked. I was beginning to believe the food I was eating was causing it, and my Doctor had no reason medically to believe I was not just suffering the normal bouts of IBS I had been diagnosed with years earlier, and becoming OCD. Becoming paranoid. He even offered to try me on Marinol, to see if perhaps that would suppress the nausea I was feeling and increase my appetite. I was a dangerously low weight. The only thing I knew for sure, was that running the studio now was incredibly stressful, and that stress did seem to be making a bad situation worse. I held out for a year, then gave in and closed it down.

Losing a dream is really hard. Shutting one down to feel better isn't. I felt the stress leave. I felt the sky open up above me. Things were better. But in all honesty, it didn't hurt so much then because I really did not understand the full ramifications of what I had just done.

Now I'm sitting here about eight years later. And my health is a bit more manageable. It turned out that the 'paranoia' that my family, friends, and doctor all thought I had about food turned out to be an extreme set of food allergies. The kind that when you eat those foods, destroy your immune system. And some of the other problems were diagnosed a short time later as Peripheral Neuropathy. But, my weight is down again, and no one really knows why. And I have new health issues, the main one being Hidradenitis Suppurativa. Don't Google image search that.

Looking back over the loss timeline I made at therapy, the problem wasn't that I shut down the studio. The problem was that I shut it down, and things did not really get better. The problem is that I also lost other opportunities because of my health, and had to walk past jobs I would be fully qualified for because I knew either the stress, or the physical expense, would make me sick again. I felt, early in this, that by giving up my dream, I would be gaining my health. I didn't realize I would lose it all, regardless.

Over the course of this experience I learned a few things, and I would like to outline them here.

1. Control

Before my health issues, I believed Human Beings had a good bit of control over their lives. Growing up, I always asked myself how folks became homeless, and the best answer I could give was "they fucked up". That is a person that believes in control, speaking.

The reality is, most of us coast along with luck. And some of us, because of the position of privilege (healthy, money, supportive environment) can coast along like this until we hit the grave, dying gracefully, as we all like to believe we will, of old age, surrounded by those who love us, and leaving behind a legacy of our contributions to this world to enrich the lives of those that follow us.

But that, is a very lucky thing. Reality is much different. And control is not part of reality. Control, I found, is an illusion. An illusion based on probabilities. What is the chance you will get cancer? Not very good, until you get it and beat it. Then those chances seem way more probable. Then you realize you do not have control.

The only thing we can control, is how we react to what life throws at us. We can go down screaming that we didn't deserve this, or we can go down holding the hands of those we care about, and loving them fully.

2. Goals

Before I got sick, I looked at goals as things you did. Set them, achieve them. Then life is better, you are better, everything is better. And I did that, but for some reason, things didn't get that much better. Something's did, I mean, making a large amount per hour will make the pain of poverty go away pretty damn quick, but it won't erase that gaping hole in your sole. You know, the one you hope to fill with fulfillment? That won't do shit for that.

You also may, in attempt to acquire the goal you know will greatly improve your existence, ruin the existence of everyone around you. You may, so blinded by your goal, turn into a complete dick. You may, become the most unmoved, uncaring, abusive asshole that you could ever become. And you may actually credit that dehumanized abusive behavior as one of your strengths, and simultaneously, learn to hate yourself and expect horrible behavior from yourself as necessary for success.

And even then, you may completely arrive at your goal, but not by way of the means and circumstance you expected, and then not be able to appreciate reaching it. And you may even walk by 1,000 other amazing things and not pay attention to them as well, simply because, they were not on your itinerary, they were not on the flight plan for your specific goal. And in doing this, you may actually work harder for your goal, as you, so devoid of seeing the beauty around you, have romanticized it into the antidote to the depressing stressful life you are currently leading. Pity anyone who should stand in the way of that.

Avoiding this behavior is rather simple: love the idea, not the specifics. And more so, love the love behind the idea: Wanting to help a specific group of people, because you care about people, seems ridiculous when you can't even take time for the one's you personally love anymore. Don't lose sight of what the core motivation is.

3. Status
Going from making $25 an hour, to $60 an hour, then down to $15, then $7.25, then basically broke and on food stamps is a humbling experience, but it's also a trying experience when related to status. Regardless of one's political or society beliefs about status, that $60 lets you know your work is appreciated. It's an instant approval of validity to your current value to the market.

The problem with this is, it is NOT a marker of your actual value to the world. To the world; your spouse, your family, your cat, your neighbors, your friends; you can add so much value that will never be capitalized on, or even be able to be figured out how to capitalize it. And we would never think of doing that, because it's "Home life", or as Thorstein Veblen termed it, 'leisure'. In the separation of our lives from work, we have deemed our marketable work as the thing that gives value. And don't believe that a leftist/anarchist does not fall for the same trap, they can value their work AGAINST the market, existing as an actual part of the market's dichotomy, as higher than what they do for friends and family.

And I shouldn't put this across as an externalized function, because as status is really just value, we can gain this from ourselves. We can feel value in what we do ourselves. But generally, we feel it for the things we love. We feel it for the things we put time into, yet don't realize how much time we've actually spent. The things that are effortless for us, because the exchange, our time for felt reward, is so lopsided to our advantage that we don't even notice how much we do.

*

In each of these things, I am a better person than when I closed down my dream studio. I realize that I have no control over anything but the way I react, and I try to react according to the life I want to live. I have loose goals that don't keep me from enjoying the journey to them. And my status, though not financially provable, is what gives me the audacity to hold my own art show, write my own book, hell, and even write this essay. I have assigned myself agency, because I know I'm valuable; a Human Being, with work that is motivated by love.

I am still very much a work-in-progress. But I like myself a lot more now than when the market/profession/industry seemed to really like me. That's a goal I would like to loosely stick to.

A NEW VALUE IN CULTURE: A RESPONSE TO 'COLLAGE CULTURE'

This essay is in response to the book 'Collage Culture', by Kahn, Rose, and Roettinger. 2011. JRP|Ringier

Through the course of human history, media has been at the hands of those with access to the machinery necessary to facilitate communication. And traditionally, these machines have been either expensive, or the knowledge required to operate them was at a specialist level. But over time, these technologies were sold to the public.

First, it was by selling to educated amateurs, those who possessed a somewhat higher level of technological prowess than the average person, usually attained through independent education. We saw this shift with the free press newspapers, the reel-to-reel four and eight track audio recorders of the early 80's, and the web of the early 90's. While these amateurs may not have produced the same quality product as a media professional could, they were able to make something passable in comparison to what was being put out by the media elite.

With the introduction of digital media, the swell of affordable digital chips and sensors, and the arrival of user friendly software for the web, we saw a democratization of media, extending production capabilities to a large chunk of the consumer market. Now the average person could produce something comparable in production quality to that of mass media products, and the savvy amateur can go head to head with the best of professional media.

For years, media has been something shown/sold/given to us. In the attempts of consumers to become producers, the only hope was to emulate/join/assimilate into the ranks of the professional media, as production required money, and only large institutions could afford it. The professional media elite were considered the 'reality' of production by us, because of the agency/value assigned to them, first by themselves with their own associations and awards, then by recognition from the owners of other elite fields and companies, and finally by us with our consent and dollar.

It was with this perspective; that of the binary world of elite producer vs. average consumer, that many of us joined in colleges, hoping to be granted agency as producers. And what were we asking to be allowed to do? To be funded. To have our visions determined important enough to receive money from the media elite, of which itself would make us elite, as there is only so much money, and only so much capacity in the traditional distribution channels for ideas. Essentially, because we wanted to produce things, we had to adopt the media elite framework, and become elite ourselves.

But, as technology has become more equal opportunity in its availability, we became able to produce and distribute our work without the big budget. Simultaneously, our system of distribution shifted our own media consumption away from the mass media system that requires big money and has finite capacity, to the distribution channels that we ourselves can publish from, shifting first with blogger journalists, then with YouTube (showing both the individual's response of the news as well as corporate media), and now with Facebook. In these frameworks, both the large institution as well as the small artist/producer/label, share the same availability, the same capacity, existing within the same format.

And in our extended capability to produce and distribute, 'Collage Culture', as termed in the book of the same name, or 'remix' culture, as Lawrence Lessig previously termed it, arises.

We had been living in a consumer culture. We looked

at the art of others, read the words of others, listened to the music of others, and watched the movies of others. This was what we 'did'. It was our mode of operation. It was our culture.

And traditionally, when we engaged ourselves in a similar field to that of the elite, like painting, writing, making music; it was treated by us, and those around us, as having a value of 'less than' that which was produced by the media elite. It was called folk art, folk music; not a memoir, but a diary. It was vernacular photography. It was home movies. It was crafts. The enormous lack of agency, IE, lack of institutional approval to assign value, to in turn, assign capital funding, and to then accrue social capital and prestige, was non-existent in these works.

And so they were treated as hobby, a term derived from the separation of work from life, and the creation of a new term, 'leisure'. We taught our kids to draw with easily erasable crayons. We taught them to finger paint. We taught them to learn the works of others in music class, and asked them to play cover songs on their guitars. We made creativity safe for them. No risk of making something lasting. And with a binary vision of regressive class consciousness, the vernacular (profane) vs. the professional (sacred), we crushed their ability to create. We told them that maybe, one day, you can be assigned agency and receive capital for your work as well. But don't count on it. Have a backup plan.

And perhaps rightfully so, as both money and distribution capacity were limited in supply to that which only a few could take advantage of. But today, it's wide open. We see the passive role of consumer, turning the media market from, as defined by the sociologist C. Wright Mills, a 'mass' situation, in which communication was a one-way action oriented from the message sender towards a body of people, into a 'public' model, where the body of people receiving a message engages in communication back with the sender of message (Mills, 1956).

Technically, there are a few reasons behind this; through the commodification of electronic components, the cost to produce is now low. With the rise and availability of the internet around the world, the capacity for distribution is ever increasing, and capital, as the critical and deciding variable in judging whether one can produce a particular media, is needed in smaller and smaller amounts to produce work. Accordingly, capital is being replaced with desire, in the requirements of production. Do you want to make a video? Do you want to write a song? Do you want to write a story? Those with passion will do it. And they will upload it to YouTube, sell it on iTunes, and post it on their blog. We are limited by what we can imagine.

'Collage culture' critiques what is made today, saying that we have begun to rehash the past. And it's true, we have. We have because, like a person who has spent much of their life forced to be silent, we are now able to speak. And we have a lot to say. So we spit back this culture, our culture, the culture of consumption, back into the eyes, ears, and collective mind of the world around us.

Remember when we were kids? Remember how lasers sounded in 80's movies? Remember the first Nintendo? Remember the crappy ROM music we thought was so awesome, and how it accompanied so many of the best days of our youth? Here they are, over a hip-hop track. Remember the late 80's, and that time my mom drove us to McDonald's, and the sun was out, the windows were down, and I saw a beautiful girl drive by with her folks, and this Phil Collins song was playing? Here is that mixed over some bass and drums. This is not a culture of copying, or simply rehashing things past. This is a culture of celebrating and subverting. Turning the mass model of communication on its head. Repossessing the culture we have been sold, and making it closer to what we really experienced, and what we actually value. And laughing at it, enjoying it.

But to do this successfully, to fully embrace the

potential of the threshold on which we currently stand, we are required to throw out all of the rules and values that were built upon the previous models of operation. And by doing so, destroy the positions of those that depend on the traditional external agency, derived from capital and finite resources and distribution capacity. Trying to value the work of any new time with the formula of the old will always prove fruitless. In this case, the past only had room for the most original of ideas, due to its limited capacity and abilities. Our new time has room for everything. Anything and everything we can imagine.

To move through this new time, we have to rebuild the way we quantify what is valuable to us. The filter, the gatekeeper of what we see, hear, and read, has moved from guarding the door of entry, to guarding the inbox, the RSS feed, the Facebook news feed, the web browser. It has moved from protecting production, to that of protecting consumption. We are now our own filters. Now we see millions of personal gatekeepers appearing; our friends or acquaintances or strangers, but of no higher agency than us, with their Tumblrs, blogs, tweets, and Facebook posts, they curate the world that appeals to them. And if we like what they show us, we choose them to be our own gatekeeper. We 'follow' them, subscribe, 'like'. Along with hundreds others, we assign them the agency of 'gatekeeper', not based on the amount of capital they have, but solely on our experience with their content.

So what are we to do in this new time of production?

If we are to judge the value of an egalitarian, open-media society, based on the rules of the old elite society, we are going to have a bad time. If we are still looking for the original idea, as pinnacle, one devoid of obvious reference, we will never move forward. Art has always been a reflection of current culture, we just were not able to physically incorporate it. So we made crude reference to it, with words, or with the brush. When Hip-hop came along, it made reference with bits of the actual preexisting idea itself, sampled, and built upon, growing an old melody into something new. And when we have exact digital representations of everything, as we do now, and in some cases, the actual digital thing itself, we must entertain the idea that we may be richer for it. That our products may be richer, more expansive. That the collage isn't a limitation of the world, but the opening of a new world.

As every medium has its boundaries, our duty is to learn the framework of the new medium, to learn what gives the new medium quality, what gives the new medium value, and where to build our work. And then, to judge it accordingly. We have to develop a literacy for the new medium. And as literacy comes with understanding, which comes with an exploration of the new medium, Art is one of the best places to explore from. Let's open ourselves to this new world and work.

But be warned; the new medium will destroy much of the style and tenants of the old. As the old media is legitimized by a system of belief conducive to its existence, the new media requires an ethic all of its own. So get ready. Evaluate what you believe is value. Re-valuate what you regard as valuable. And be ready to adapt to the new framework.

And while moving forward, instead of holding the values of old as our currency, be ready to change what we assign worth to. And for the sake of everyone involved, let's make that currency be based upon something that is human in quality, and caters to the world we dream of living in. Perhaps, referencing compassion, rather than scarcity.

Citation:
Mills, C. Wright 'The Power Elite' pg. 320-8. Oxford Press. 1956.

A TALE OF MODERN BUSINESS

Brands are seen as the most valuable asset a company has. The reason? The brand represents the vision of the company behind a brand. Accordingly, as a vision, the reality of experiences with a company may or may not match the vision, much like the believers of a religion may or may not meet the demands of their religion. In business, the brand is the religion.

Happy Co.

Let's say there is a company called Happy Co. The company was made up of some people, and like most people, they were some pretty decent folks. They were formed by two of these people. These two people had a vision a while back to try and make a new tool, one that they though would change, or at least enhance, the world. And they had a way to make it a profitable product. And it was a very decent product. The market already had similar products, but not quite the way these folk's products were. Happy Co. made a product that was different. Not starkly different. But a little different. What they needed was a way to convey, explicitly, that this was a different product; IE, product differentiation.

The way they used to do this, you made an Ad explaining the product. That's the way we do it now as well, but we also make an Ad explaining the brand. Instead of arguing that this product is indeed better every single time, make the argument that Happy Co is better, and there for every product of Happy Co is better.

Of course, we are all as different as people, maybe it's a better product for you but not for me. This is market segmentation. So Happy Co has to sit down and figure out, who is our core customer? How can we make exactly what they need, or at least more of what they need than anyone else?

They hire a firm to research their core customer. Perhaps sales have been slipping, and they realize their core customer isn't their ideal customer. Perhaps they've been running too many sales, and their core customer's only allegiance to the brand is based on the low prices they offer. Happy Co wants to increase profit, and isn't in a position to lower production costs just yet, so in order to grow to a point where they could build in mass at a rate sufficient to lower costs, they decide they need to raise their prices.

The research firm says that this will lose their current customer base, and that they will need to find a new one. The research firm shows Happy Co statistics they have gathered on new markets that seem to be on the rise, in particular, niche markets. The downside of a niche market is you have relegated yourself to one demographic of sales. The upside is that if you meet the needs of this niche market, you may have a core customer base of supreme dedication to your brand. Like a man who brings food to the starving, Happy Co would be the first group to take these customer's needs seriously. They would respect Happy Co for that, and probably buy more of their products.

Happy Co takes a few days to think about this. While they do like turning a profit, and the sales they have run have had that effect, it seems that overtime, and the sales have been being undercut by other business doing the same. And they were bigger businesses, business that could buy product in large enough quantities to influence supply costs, and actually lower those costs for the products they buy and sell. So $1 at their competitor might mean $0.58 profit, whereas at Happy Co, it meant $0.18 of profit.

And in talking to the research firm, the founders of Happy Co reminisced of the reasons they went into business in the first place. To sell their product, sure, but also to do it in a way that benefitted other people's lives. To make the world a better place. Even if just a little better, from the time saved using Happy Co.'s product. The company thought about it, and then made a decision. They would take the leap.

Research firms for business gather lots of data. They do this by doing consumer tests. Through trial and error, test panels, and surveys, the research firms know a bit about how people buy the things they do, and why. Understanding the 'why' and the 'how' means that the firm can offer a business insight into how a type of customer shops, and why they shop, allowing the business to tailor their sales floor and product inventory to one that reflects what the customer wants.

Traditionally customer expectation has been handled the GM way. Make a bad-ass, top tier car, the Cadillac, then incorporate bits of that Cadillac into every lower model, down to the base model. This has worked for many companies, and is still in use today. And it works very well.

But the founders of Happy Co. always resented the upsell model. They were more utilitarian folks. They believed a tool should be a tool, and get out of the way and let you work. So, with the help of the research firm, Happy Co rebranded itself as a simple company.

They decided to limit their current product offering down to just a few items. For some products, there were specific features that some customers may want, but other customers might not need. So they made a 'good' and a 'damn-good' version. For other items that were more utilitarian, they just made one. Maybe you could pick a specific color, or maybe not. The research firm gave advice on colors.

The other area would be their stores. Happy Co stores looked like any other store of their industry, and suffered the same pitfalls. The research firm had tons of data on floor sales and customer psychology in retail settings. They urged Happy Co. to extend the new simplicity of its inventory to its retail stores. Happy Co had traditionally carried products by other companies alongside their own, especially accessories. But the research firm said that by doing that, Happy Co was admitting there are equal options to their own products, in their own store. That would seem to customers as though these other products offered something that Happy Co could not offer themselves. It would seem as a failure of Happy Co.

Happy Co. thought about it. For some items, accessories was the biggest sales item. They said they could not do away with the accessories. The research firm looked at their data and realized keeping accessories may actually bring some customers back to Happy Co after the initial purchase. So accessories stayed in. But for big items, like items that competed with Happy Co, they had to go. Happy Co. products alongside other brand name brands made Happy Co. appear to be a store-brand, usually the equated with discount merchandise in the eyes of shoppers. Happy Co decided to make its products a brand-name brand themselves, and use their stores to stand behind them as validation of this.

And so, armed with a new inventory and a new sales list, Happy Co and the research firm set about re-building Happy Co. The first order was to take what it had discovered from its products, and build a visual language around the company, one that said "Happy Co" when a customer saw it, though not literally. They decided on a vision: "to make great products that make people happy". They hired a design firm to go through some of the color schemes that the research firm had determined capable of making folks happy, and a new color scheme was created. The crown jewel, a new logo, was also designed, tied into the color scheme. The research firm tested the new color scheme and logo on customer test groups. They asked people what the logo made them feel. The firm was shooting for two words, "safe" and "happy". They made some changes to the logo until tests provided good results. They even built a test store, and brought customers in to observe how they responded to it. After a few weeks, the framework of the new Happy Co was in place.

(Note: If this were a high quality production, or if I felt so inclined, you would see here two images. One would be of the Happy Co children's area before branding, featuring a man displaying a pistol next to a child. The child is crying. The next image would be of a child holding a much nicer, funner, happier looing pistol. Smiling. Yes, Happy Co manufactures firearms.)

The research firm and the designers compiled a new manual for Happy Co operations, designed in the livery of the new Happy Co. The company managers were excited. After so many years of the old 'brand', they were ecstatic to have an environment around them that actually attested to the things they believed about Happy Co. They felt purpose on the sales floor. They felt part of a good organization. They believed in their company again.

Happy Co. set a transition date for its stores and brand, and set up the logistics to make the transition occur gracefully. It would happen on September 12 at 12:00 AM. Temporary trailers were given to drivers the days before so the company-owned trailers could be wrapped in the new graphics. Deliveries that day would be made in the newly wrapped trailers. The store managers spent the week having fire sales of inventory clearing out everything for the new merchandise. A crane truck sat idly by the entrance to company headquarters, next to the cloth draped frame of the new signage. Employee clothing was shipped to the stockrooms instructing the employees to not open them until 12 AM.

When 11:45PM came, all the mangers appeared at the stores all across the country. Corporate had a man from the company come out to each store to assist. At midnight, every Happy Co store across the country was filled with the sound of moving display cases, electric drills, and the soft thump of rubber mallets knocking cabinets into place. Eventually they drowned in echo as the store floors became empty. And then the wheels of dolleys squeaked across the country; the new pallets being hauled in from the back. Soon it was a symphony of box cutters and the clack of metallic things being set down upon fresh melamine. At corporate; the crane balanced the sign, illuminated with floodlights, and the canvas cover was pulled off. Happy Co. had been reinvented.

Sales that week were peculiar. While the newspapers had run feature stories about the launch of the new happy co (at the advice of the research firm), the public wasn't 'fully engaged' with new brand. But things like this take some time. Winning people's trust, the ultimate goal of every brand, takes time. And convincing old customers that you are something different now, customers who may have been loyal more to price than to core vision, takes time. A drop in sales was seen. The research firm had warned Happy Co of all of this, as stepping foot in a specific direction means stepping away from another. But the company made the decision to stick to it, despite the fears of some internally. And then March happened.

Happy Co usually rolled out products when they were available, no hoopla, no big-time press releases, but on the heels of the newspaper stories about the businesses rebranding, and the public interest in the dramatic quickness it occurred, many eyes were on Happy Co. So when it came time to release what would be one of their new, streamlined core-products, they played up the fanfare. They hit the press in cities they had stores, they went on television showing the cameras around the way the new stores worked, and they showcased their new product in magazines, as something important. Not just another tool. But THE tool. A specific tool. A tool for people who wanted to be both "safe" and "happy".

Public Interest was piqued. The press set itself ablaze with speculation about whether the brand would actually meet the expectations being put on it by the media. Business critics lauded the company, some saying it should have even been shut down. But most media remained positive, almost disconnected in expectation, just enjoying the novelty of the spectacle that was occurring around such a particular product.

Release day was met with enthusiasm. Management came to the stores to oversee the affair. Not only was the product part of the brand of Happy Co, but the way it was sold had to be as well. "We can't make people Happy, if they are unhappy with the way they had to purchase it", said Mike Kenner, VP of Retail Operations. In an unheard of move, cashiers took the purchase lines with handheld point-of-sale devices, ringing up customers while they stood in line. Staff then brought the product, already bagged, to the waiting customers. The lines dissipated quickly, and by the end of the day, the sales numbers were tallied. Management could not believe it. Not only had sales surpassed the numbers of any of the industry-specific competitors, but they had surpassed those of all retail business in their respective shopping complexes. It was thought, that they might have even surpassed the numbers of every individual retailer in the entire country. Happy Co. brand transition, had been justified.

Over the next few years, Happy Co grew and grew.

And as it did, it purchased from lower and lower levels in the supply chain, growing to the point where it had significant influence on the cost of the materials it was purchasing. Leveraging this power, Happy Co could bring things to market cheaper than other companies could afford to do. So even when it priced itself a little above the competition, say 10%, the price the quality of its brand allowed them to do, they could make a 90% profit, whereas its competitor could only retain 30-50%. Some materials where purchased in such great supply that the cost to all buyers, and all competitors, actually decreased, due to the increased effort and infrastructure dedicated to producing them. In other cases, the exact opposite effect happened; their quantity purchases left less of the resource available, driving costs up for everyone, including Happy, who only discounted by buying so many at one time.

They found themselves in a unique position, one where the conglomerated auto companies had found themselves years before. Because of their purchasing power, they could build a high quality product, relatively cheap. If they were willing to sacrifice a bit of their profit margin, they could extend the mission of Happy Co and the benefits of owning a Happy Co product, to those that had been decidedly left out of their market. The founders considered it. Perhaps the old upsell model, trickling down features to the most inexpensive model, wasn't a bad idea. The research firm agreed this would give them the ability to 'sell the middle', a strategy of bringing rational folks in on discounts, then leading them to buy the more feature filled models. Or for the more monetarily challenged, to be able to own a piece of the high-end model, much like a smaller, high- quality home to the new urbanists, or conversely, a cake crumb to the communists.

Regardless of interpretation, it meant Happy Co had the power to really change the world. They set out to prepare some prototypes, and after revisions and a numbers session with their manufacturing and finance guys, decided to embark on making a product everyone could afford.

From here, Happy Co made history. A history that crowned its founders as geniuses, it's designers as sages, and the marketing firm with a higher per-hour billing rate. And it filled the homes of many folks with lots of Happy Co products. Almost anywhere you looked, from the street corner, to business world, Happy Co was in full view.

But as time moved on, its founders moved on. Spurred by the access of money and opportunities, they ventured into different areas of life. Both still passionate about making folks feel both "happy" and "safe", they found other industries prime for their talents. One in medicine, the other in automobiles. As they both waned their interests, talk of selling the company began to appear in their conversations.

On March 3, 2018, almost 9 years after releasing their first hit product, the product that defined the success and direction of the company, Happy Co was sold to Cegal Inc., a family-owned company that owned many successful brands, including a few of Happy Co.'s competitors. The founders, appearing at a last product launch, expressed their thanks to the millions of people that had made Happy Co a success, and wished the company well in its future. The company would never be the same again.

Sure, they've had good products since then. But the drive was gone. That once legendary attention to detail, the highly supportive customer support, the strategic innovation, knowing that whatever would come release day WOULD be amazing, was not so amazing now, but more Ho-hum. As the company suffered small losses in sales, the new owners moved people around a bit, and when things started heading down hill, brought in their best people from the other companies they owned. But nothing seemed to work.

The problem was, Happy Co was a zebra. And it had

to be sold to customers as a zebra.

And in a market filled with horses and donkeys, you cannot try to sell a zebra as a horse. Only a fool would try to sell a zebra as a horse. What the Happy Co-founders discovered was, you have to sell the Zebra as the animal the horses where all trying to be, and in turn, failing to be. And so they succeeded. Cegal were horse men. They had owned horses of every size, and knew how to make horses perform. So they treated Happy Co as a horse. And it almost bucked like one. But then it died.

Ten years later, Happy Co was sold to Brands United, a company that buys brands that once had strong draw, and tries to reinvigorate them, at least well enough to sell subpar merchandise under its logo. And that's where it sits today. It's kind of sad, knowing where it came from.

LEARNING TO STAND AS ME

I was once asked by a man, why I was not at war right now.

The question struck me of something that would have been asked 60 years ago, but with this man's age, I could figure that this was the same question he may have been asked when he was younger. It had been kept in a bottle in his mind. And when it was asked, it's mustiness, aged by its fevered jingoist implications, and dated by its assumption that all men should willing to kill for their country, sat thick in the air, pierced only by my wide-eyed amazement.

I explained that I lost a friend in Iraq, to which he told me my friend had 'done a good thing', and suggested I do the same.

I left this conversation feeling broken. Like I had been punched in the face. Like everything I've done in my life, every little thing I have made, in attempts to make the world better for those in it, were crushed and grinded under an all too familiar boot. The boot of my old friend, the idealistic soldier I dreamed of being when I was 10.

I used to want to fight for the United States. I grew up

playing war. I had my toy soldiers. I had my toy guns. When the toys didn't suffice, I had my mother take me to surplus stores and obtained the standard issued clothing. I had joined the cub scouts as soon as I was old enough, and then the boy scouts, and enjoyed many of our military centered events. An overnight sleepover on an aircraft carrier. Midnight games of laser tag in the gymnasium at Fort Bragg. Digging terraces for the Army Corps of Engineers. Seeing the soldiers and climbing all over their Helicopters at the National Jamboree. And learning to shoot rifles.

At about 11, I remember riding back from the surplus store, and it occurred to me, that 'killing' meant I would be 'killing' actual people. Having grown up a southern Baptist, and ever-loving to human beings, especially the faceless mass idea of human beings, I asked my mother, 'how can soldiers kill?' This followed with 'But isn't it Murder?', 'Does God excuse soldiers?' My mother, being one of the most compassionate Human Beings I have ever known, as well as a devout Christian, replied that she did not know how they could be excused. That killing is always wrong. I accepted this quickly. And with that, decided that if I should ever join the military, it would be as a chaplain.

When I became a teenager, I found punk rock. And the moral question I had asked earlier, became concretely backed up by the lyrics of dozens of bands. For the first time, I had found an intellectual framework, based on reason and rational argument, against the killing. The songs against the violence, that highlighted the hypocrisy inherent in the military solution of fixing world problem through killing people, became my favorite. And in finding this, the wounds left of justifying my idea of good; God, with the idea of a world built by him that viewed killing as acceptable; an obvious attack on all Living Beings, was healed. But I also realized something quite unsettling; that the majority of the people around me in this society, profess a morality that they contradict, and adamantly contradict, daily. In this realization, many of my heroes died instantly. And a new world view was created, based on the idea that our adherence to our morality was the quality to be admired, and that the morality I admire and strive for, is one that respects ALL living beings.

I set about to sew my own seeds of support those people who had a spirit like mine. I attempted it in lyric, I attempted it in action, and I attempted it at the core of my being. And for the most part I succeeded; I created many songs over the years that focus on that hypocrisy, and give reverence to those that resist it, and those that build alternatives. I gave support from whatever power I've had, that of organizations I was a part of, or the power inherent in myself, to causes that furthered a resistance to the obliteration of human being through instruments of power, be it bombs or poverty. But in my own life, I failed. Over and Over again.

Growing up I was attacked. A lot. I was an outsider. I reflected on the world around me. My childhood years consisted of a back and forth see-saw of trying to be accepted, and rejecting the need to be accepted. My attempts at being accepted rang false to my peers. It resulted in a lot of teasing, and a lot of bullies trying to kick my ass. I could not wear a polo shirt right. I could not wear a baseball cap right. I have a picture of myself, age 11 or so at the Boy Scout jamboree, with my hat broken off to the side. I just could not let myself fit in. I'd spend hours decorating my bicycle like my favorite motorcycle, fashioning logos and even a top tank out of a paper bag, and the neighborhood bullies would rip them apart. My friends would not acknowledge me in the presence of other they looked up to. I was trying to be friends with the 'good kids', and I rang false to them. And I was being false. I think the ultimate problem was, I was very compassionate, and I was very smart. And those two things mean one thing to the average male kid: faggot.

So I would decide to be me. The loving, smart, kid, who had compassion. And I would get attacked. But I would fight back. This lead to folk's families calling my family, asking why I threatened to kick the ass of their son, who had threatened me. Asking why I had chucked a chunk of ice in a snowball fight, at the face of a kid who was making fun of me. Asking why I was running around the neighborhood, without a shirt on, at 8 years old, carrying a bb gun. All fair questions. But mostly ignoring, and even supporting the fact, that their child had bullied me. I remember one parent saying that I shouldn't threaten her son, that it was his right to want to beat me up, and she couldn't stop him from doing it, because I'm weak and probably deserve it. This was my suburban life.

Add to this domestic patriarchal physical violence and mental abuse at home, and you had a kid that was in a hell of a quandary. To be compassionate, to be caring, to challenge the status quo of non-compassion and violence as a young smart kid I had to be strong. Very strong. I had to be ready for abuse. I had to be ready for violence.

And I had to become my own advocate. I remember a local radio station had gotten a hold of my bands demo tape. They were playing it, then pausing and making fun of each line of my lyrics. To a 14 year-old kid who had trusted in the value of music as a safe, cathartic space, this was the worst nightmare. I listened in horror, as the most honest confessions of my emotional life were ripped to shreds by college kids on college radio. My friends and I called the station and told them, in so many words, that we were not happy about this and they may want to take care with themselves. In one of many other episodes, I was issued a death threat in a zine by kid who was going off to join the Marines, whom did not appreciate my anti-war stance. And this kind of thing went on and on. So I became used to the idea of being violent, in defense of myself, as a necessary condition of my existence. I found family in punk rock, and in that family I found people who would stand next to me through thick and thin, and fight for me. They were my crew. And through this was more violence.

I also had to create my own self-esteem. Growing up as I did, I had no clue as to any intelligence I had. I functioned one of two ways in school; either on honor roll, or failing. Never in between. I concluded I was an idiot, probably helped on that by those around me, save for my Mother, had concluded I was an idiot. So I did as an idiot would do, and clung to the only things that seemed to work. Skateboarding. Guitar. Then punk rock. In punk I found self-esteem. In meeting a friend, he showed me that I had value, in all aspects of my life. That I was a good person. Then he was killed. And I went on half-knowing I was good, amidst a sea of negative to non-existent affirmation. So I realized if anyone was going to acknowledge my good qualities, it would be me. During the months where I was lowest, where I needed that affirmation greatly, I had to generate it myself. And accordingly would come off cocky. And when it was the worst, I would come off completely egotistical.

And then it hit its toll. I found myself in a relationship where my violence, born as a protection to the external world, was now corroding my life. I was having an impossible time correlating between the love in my heart, and the necessary protection needed for such caring. And that juxtaposition, made me feel that the necessary conditions needed to protect that good, made that good something that I unconsciously shied away from. Good became corroded by the reality of what I felt I needed to do to protect it. And the ego boosting much needed from feeling like such a failure to obtain the feeling of ever being good enough, let alone the high idealism I had been shooting for in much of my life, meant I was constantly rationalizing myself, and being cocky, falling upon deaf ears and jaded eyes.

And I hurt those that I loved.

And then a friend died in Iraq. And for once, I paid attention to reality. I questioned a lot of things during that time, but one thing in particular was my actions. I realized that words and actions themselves will lead us to a certain life. And it will be the product of the actions and words involved in it, regardless of the intent, or the desired end goal. That violence ahead of the idea of compassion will end up the same way a soldier fighting a war, not for grand nationalism, but for the reasons of his own personal situation, will end up; in violence and death. And I tried to be present with that. And I tried to end those years of suffering. It ended up with my life falling apart at the seams, and a trip to a mental hospital.

The ensuing recovery was a rebuilding. A new city to thrash old mental patterns. Being single to force me to find my way myself. A new job to help rebuild my foundations and confidence. And over time I built my strength up, this time open-palmed instead of closed-fist, with humility instead of hardened resolve, and I began to build what I would call 'my life'. This time, in the shape of the one I had always wanted: full of love, compassion, and understanding. Acting decidedly as an adult, leaving behind the abused kid who had to fight everyone just to stand still.

And so, looking back on the question of that old veteran, asked to me at a time when I had rebuilt myself to live decidedly, and with purpose in the pursuit of compassion and non-violence, I'm amazed by it still. Why am I not killing people in the specific name of one nation? Because as a living being, it is the absolute worst thing I could ever do. I would be betraying my kind. And it would corrode my life and the life of those around me, especially of those that I killed, and it would set a horrific moral standard for human behavior when added back to the cumulative course of human action. The only thing I could do worse, would be to then be proud of it.

I should have asked "to what end?" So that men can keep on controlling other men through mechanisms of power, leveraged either by the violence of war or the violence of debt? A violence that sews mistrust and abuse into the lives of those it touches to the point where they feel they have to take to violence to perpetuate something as beautiful as the love and compassion they want for their families and themselves?

Taking careful consideration of the situation of this question, I regret not saying any of this to that man. But I did not know any of this. I was bowled over with the reverence I felt to those that gave their lives for the idea of our nation, and not comfortable standing on the feet of myself as a human being who rejects this. It was because I still viewed the act of death for a cause, and the power of a gun as being more legitimate than those whom sew a culture that works to carry forth the beauty of life, for all humans, regardless of nation or political belief.

But I know it now. And I won't forget it. I won't forget that for each of us that makes a stand, towards a hopeful future, that each of us carries forth a moral currency to which our intent never escapes the sum of our actions. And that those actions should be taken wholly, as the way we have chosen to conduct our lives. When we take that approach, we will never mistake violence as justified, and more widely, as serving a goal of humanity. When we take that approach, the totality of our being will stand equal to the totality of our ethics. Until then, we will fail our idealism.

Unpublished

MOTIVATIONS FOR ACTIONS

I've been thinking a lot lately about our motivations for actions: Why we do things? Is it because we want to share it? Are excited about it? Want to find out more about it? Or is it because we want to brag to the world about it?

I've become hyper vigilant about making sure my motivations are closer to the sharing, rather than the bragging.

Why should we care about bragging?

Well, at some level, bragging exploits scarcity; I have this, and you don't. Such behavior leverages the mechanisms that create scarcity in order to create the condition where bragging has the desired effect. When you realize that those mechanisms include wealth, meritocracy, and ability, we realize that bragging sets out to condemn a person for their perceived 'lower' current position, which probably isn't so much a product of their own doing, so much as an averaging of the external forces they make trade with every day.

That is troubling to me. But luckily I've been reading a good bit about intentions in my Non-Violence class I am currently taking.

Gandhi believed strongly in not the product of actions, but the intention behind it. This is something I've gone over in the dichotomy of process vs. product that I've been toying with for a while.

And in toying with it, I mean I've been trying to live by example. Love the day as much as the date. Love the preparation as much as the meal. Realize that the fruits of our labor (the product) are the PRODUCT of process, and the disassociation of the two leads to trouble, especially for humans, as we spend our lives in the process. The process is our quality of life. The product of our lives, in total, is something we will never experience. Becoming comfortable with that requires letting go of ego-driven desires, yet somehow still remaining active.

A lot to think about.

LOST IN THE CHASE

My super awesome ex-wife found these vacuum tubes the other day while cleaning and dropped them off with me. Looking at them, I was reminded of the way life worked when I was younger.

The way it worked was this: Chase.

Something not working right? Chase down the solution. Chase it down at night. Chase it down during the day. Chase it down all year. Better yet, chase better, chase smarter, in some hope that it may lead to less chasing in the long run.

The problem? After about three or four years of chasing things down, you realize that, sometime while you were chasing, life happened. And all you are left with is some misgivings about what you could have done, and two little pieces of glass that may be worth something to people whom are chasing as well.

I got lost in the chase, and it's like a zero sum game for folks that cannot be present.
As a new father, I hope I spend the least amount of time lost in the chase as possible, and the most amount of time present, with my spouse and daughter, being a

helpful person in their lives.

And it's not just about chasing vacuum tubes that mean something to people on eBay. It's also about not getting lost chasing other things; songs, art, hell, even blog posts like this about not getting lost in things. As I'm sitting here, my daughter let me know she needed me, and I left, tended to her, and am back. Someone lost in the chase would have asked for a few more minutes to not break the train of thought.

Why do we get lost in the chase?

I think its fear. Fear of our train of thought getting derailed, and lack of confidence in our ability to resume it later. And perhaps, a crushing need of validation now, heaped on top of it.

These are difficult waters to navigate, and this navigation is something I struggle with daily. Perhaps I will write a little more about it as I encounter more examples that pop up.

THOUGHTFULLNESS / MIDBRAIN RESPONSE

There is an 'autopilot' nature to much of life. The point where mid-brain response kicks in, and we just 'do'. I think this evolved so we could provide for ourselves when we are tired; make breakfast, change our baby, gather food, etc. It's a part of life, and I see nothing wrong with this.

Certain things in our world today tap into that process. TV is one, a lot of social media is another. The catch is we end up negotiating interactions with others, and many of the interactions of our lives, in more of a mid-brain response pattern, than in a thoughtful, and conscious method.

I see some definite downsides to this. My feeling is that a lot of what we see in terms of negativity on the internet, is a product of this less-thoughtful, mid-brain response cycle; responding to others without giving so much thought to something. Not out of lack of ethics, but simply because of manipulation of process, by being in environments, physical or mental, that cater to eliciting mid-brain response.

It's also interesting to consider where we create in these

methods: things like integral, where we can take a picture and share it with a few movements of a wrist and finger, means we are viewing much more content that may be created by the mid-brain response. When we consider that the mid-brain response is a product of training, based on repeated action, we can begin to see the problem with this. Status quo stands a higher chance of being represented in response, based purely on incidence of exposure. Also things like fear, which may not lead to reposes that coincide with what we consciously believe ethically, or morally.

In short, this response caters to a reality we have known, rather a reality we decidedly want to exist. And when we realize we are building many interactions in our world based on situations that elicit midbrain response, there is cause to worry about regression from ideals, or perpetuation of the cycles that condition midbrain response.

EXPLORING THE SONG: 'FOLDED FLAG'

In 2005, a man I grew up with was killed in the Iraq war. I grew up with him via High School and punk rock, and he was a friend of my closest friends. I had never experienced loss of a person I had known to war, and so the experience was an awakening.

His death, personalized me to the term "we". As in its use of "We", the United States. I had been working in businesses, living as a citizen, and electing folks to office, all in the hopes that my efforts would support what I wanted to see in the world: More peace.

All of a sudden the "We" went beyond the academic or logical admissions of failure that "We" as a people, had made on the fronts of working towards peace, and now admitted a complicity and a responsibility in the actions of our government, that now resulted in a personally connected loss. On that day I began to see politics, and its essential nature of arguing over points of view, as not ever worth human suffering.

I wrote a song about it called 'Folded Flag' a few months later. I released it the following year on the "This Malaise Is Our Grave" EP, as F*BOX. It's seems simple and benign on the outside, through no intention of mine, but I will pull back the lyrics a bit to explain them at each line.

(NOTE: I'm not including my friends name here, as I would not want to exploit his family or name for my view of what happened. These lyrics are how I interpreted the event. And accordingly, should not affect his family's memory of his life or intentions. I went back and forth numerous times of if it was even appropriate to write a song about. In the end, I decided I could document my reaction to it. I understood why he signed up, and as all I ever knew of him was that he was a very good person, with very good intentions. And it pains me, as I know it does others, that he is gone. RIP man.)

"She's been sleeping, since the morning we failed to wake / Responsibility we failed to take"
The morning of 9/11, and the days following, America was filled with compassion for those that lost their lives. I hoped that we might awake to the realization that fighting wars leads to more wars. That was why, after all, someone had chosen to attack us: The attacker viewed our violence against them as worthy of an attack. And the attacker had actually been trained by us years ago to help fight our mutual enemies. But we decided to wage another war, in the hopes that we might bring peace. And so the most powerful nation in

the world, fed back into the cycle of violence that has plagued Mankind since its earliest years.

"Our dreams are recursive / we fight the battle we already fought / loose more life each time we've lost".
This was our second war with Iraq. Why Iraq? Ask Colin Powell, despite Saddams' son in law, Hussein Kamel al-Majid, whom had defected years before, and had made a statement that all WMD's were destroyed previously, and knew this as he was leader of the WMD program, and CIA confirmed this.

And still, we went back to war.

The allusion to war as a dream draws upon the presence of War on TV like CNN, where war is turned into decontextualized, non-real time sound bites, usually with a different narrative, not much different than a dream. And as I view all war as promoting war, I believe each time we decide to fight, we have lost the battle for peace.

"Is anyone keeping score anymore / cuz I can't see from the photo but I swear I keep losing my friends".
This is in response to General Tommy Frank's statement that "We don't do body counts", the famous remark he made when questioned how many Iraqi civilians had been killed, which at the time was

estimated in the hundreds of thousands. The second line is in reference to the infamous rule the US instituted during the war, blocking of photographers from the area of Dover Airbase where the caskets, or flag-draped "transfer cases" of soldiers whom have died in combat are unloaded.

"The cemetery is filled with the dead / like a sea of marble flowing to the edge".
That's the visual image I remember of Arlington National Cemetery, where my friend was buried.

"Republican Blue / Someone's waiting blood, Democrat Red / What we've left behind / it's all the same, on a folded flag".
These are references to waiting blood, and blood spilled. And that waiting blood, blue with patriotism, and an honest belief in defending this country as a good thing. Though I feel differently, I respect the beliefs of those willing to fight wars. The sad part is that in this war, perhaps some of that intention may have been influenced by the lies that led us into Iraq.

Also, the idea is that both parties, regardless of position on other issues, both fought for the war. Very few stood up and asked for a moment to consider other options. And perhaps that has to do with all politicians wanting to seem strong, and the western view of Anti-Violence as a position of weakness.

And the flag part, well, watching my friend's ex and son receive that flag really stuck with me, especially with the all that was happening. In that moment all that seemed to matter in the world was that someone had lost their life. It was really focused and powerful.

Additionally, as I had not noted much of formal politics, I remembered the party colors wrong, blame Bush's propensity for wearing blue ties, I figured they were his colors. My sister noted this before I released the song, but I figured it was somewhat Freudian in my opinion that both parties are essentially the same.

(repeat)

Then the song repeats. Because, while this was the first time such a tragedy has played out in my life, it is just part of a cycle of violence that has effected millions of folks, and will continue to until we begin to see actions and intent as more important than the lines or policies we have divided ourselves by.

THOUGHTS ON NSA REVELATIONS

I'd like to talk a little about the recent leak that confirmed the NSA has been monitoring American conversations.

I have been concerned for a while now about the concentration of private data into a few corporate hands. This prompted me to start Responsible Analytics in 2008, and has been responsible for my own fickleness with depending on accounts with these large companies. Even without the NSA peeping in, just the corporate exploitation of this data should be worrisome enough.

This issue hinges around the expectation of Privacy by the average citizen. Did citizens signing up for Facebook, Gmail, Yahoo Mail, Hotmail, expect their "private" email and messaging to be accessed by NSA? The law has defined privacy as the "Reasonable Expectation" a citizen would have, so whether it's a violation should be judged by that.

The recent CNN poll claiming 56% of Americans support the NSA's actions: I'm not surprised, but I am saddened. I believe the American public does not understand the long standing privacy implications of this action being deemed acceptable, nor understand the legal, technical, and business implications for both Americans and the rest of the world, in NSA being able to monitor these systems. But as Congress itself has been slow to understand anything remotely technical, I am not surprised other people have a hard time.

But I do understand it, and over the years, I have spent a lot of time thinking, reading, and talking with folks about this type of thing, here are my thoughts:

Our digital devices track everything about us. Saying its OK for anybody to collect data from them destroys our potential for any privacy, ever. It means the choice will be 1) technology or 2) privacy. I believe the rational choice would be a middle ground between the two, much like what most Americans probably believed they were making when they purchased these devices. The reality is that, today the choice is, as Neil Postman put it, a Faustian bargain, trading privacy for technology. And while that is up to each of us to make, what about those, like me, whom have a school email account I am required to use, run by a company whom gives the NSA access to its system? Where is my choice? It is to either go to school, or have privacy. No one in a "free" country should ever have to make that choice.

It puts at risk citizens of all nations to surveillance by US Intelligence. Why care about that? It means that future web companies (like Facebook, Google, Yahoo) will have big incentives to not start their businesses here in the US, as doing so will subject their worldwide user base to the surveillance of one nation. This is a huge issue. It also means the sales of devices that depend on these services, will extend such tradeoffs when they are purchased. This then retards society from technology and creates a new class of users, those with the tech will be those willing to trade away privacy. In an evolutionary sense, it means future products and services would be more willing to trade more of the same. Bye Bye Choice, Bye Bye Freedom.

Letting the NSA collect data violates our rules that the military cannot be used domestically against citizens. The NSA is not the FBI. They are military in nature, and military in technology. This is the digital equivalent to an M1 Abrams tank, an armed apache helicopter, coming into our cities daily. When the FBI, a police operation, wants to tap something, they have to do it in a small, targeted scale. It requires warrants, it requires effort. In short, it is closer to the letter of the law. What NSA is doing, would technically require martial law to be declared in order to fully do it legally. This should concern the hell out of anyone who likes the constitution.

I'm sure I will have more thoughts about this in the future. I'd just like to close saying this: I believe the goal of a government should be to enable its citizens to enjoy a good, free, life. That means doing work that enables opportunities for its citizens, that creates a fertile ground in both rights and economic opportunity for imagination to be indulged, and dreams to be realized, among all of its people. And I don't see the NSA's actions to be in line with that at all.

RING DIAGRAMS OF OPERATION MOTIVES

A few days ago, I was graphing some of the things I've been working on, trying to figure out what realms they address. I came up with four categories 1) Self 2) Imagination 3) Knowledge 4) Commerce. In trying to plot them, I drew them in these rings, operating outwardly.

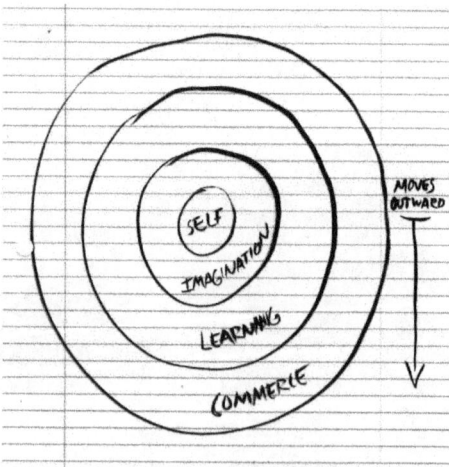

The idea is that the outer ring consists of the inner ring, and the outer ring adds to the inner ring.

Interesting as a model, not sure how provable. Then I flipped it...

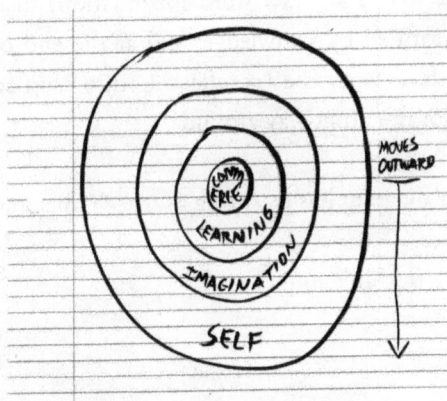

Is this not what the worst-case scenario of consumerism looks like?

I was struck by this as I was watching a documentary about Instagram, and seeing how the service/product has allowed people be creative in a space, but it ends up centering back on the product. This reminds me of how Neil Postman said that technology always ends up serving itself, its propagation and survival is its first job, uber alles.

And it's precisely this flow that has driven me to delete dozens of Facebook, Myspace, Flickr, and other social network accounts. I don't like serving products under the guise of 'creativity'. To me creativity is fucking sacred, and should only be gone about for serving the rings in order of the first diagram, to establish self-awareness, feed and draw from imagination, to build and be informed by knowledge, and at the end of the road, perhaps can be condensed into something salable. Not the other way around.

This latter diagram has us sitting as true "Consumers".

Something to think about.

PRODUCTION AS FEEDBACK LOOPS

Would you like to see the biggest failure of Humanity?

It's what is pictured in the picture above.

For a long while, the way human beings have tended to create has been from source, to product, then product comes back to nature, in a way that is not reclaimable by nature. Hence it's a one way system. And that gap in the circle above, that what we refer to as "externalization", where things go to die. Out of sight. Out of mind. But not in a way in accordance with the reality of the natural world.

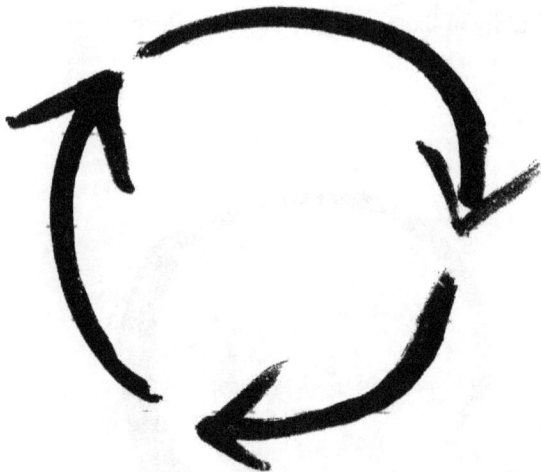

When the recycle movement came to fruition, the recycle arrow attended to the way we use things in society, produce, consume, re-use, hence the three point arrow.

Our current society hinges on the idea of use, as a separate step of a product. And I think it's this mindset, itself a product of the one way system of use it grew from, that holds us back from making further progress. I think subtly, a new language must appear that is not part of the 'use' paradigm.

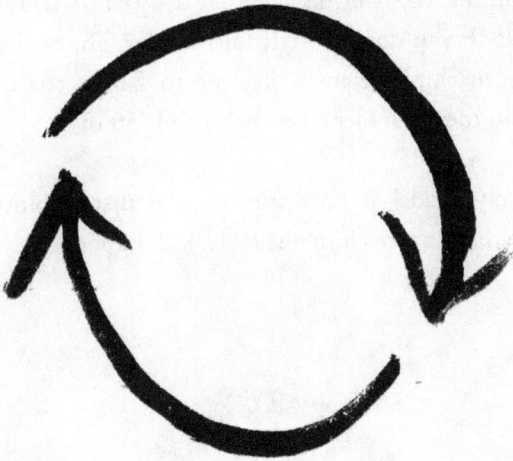

When I discovered this idea, it was in the framework of engines. Rather than designing engines that 'use', to achieve real progress, we must strive for engines that just produce and build upon, like a feedback loop. So two stages, build, build upon, kind of like a turbo, but without external input in the cycle. (Gasoline injection)

Different Application: When a car exists, it spends its life in one of three stages: 1) Production 2) Use 3) Decay. The decay stage is looked at as when the car is junked. My view is that there are only two stages 1)

Production 2) Product. And the decay stage is inherent in the product stage. After all, when can we really decide the car is in decay? After a certain amount of miles? IF you don't drive it for months? The reality is, every machine begins a journey to falling apart the second the assembler takes their hands off of it.

But my model is only true for the first revolution. After that, it turns into one cycle, build upon.

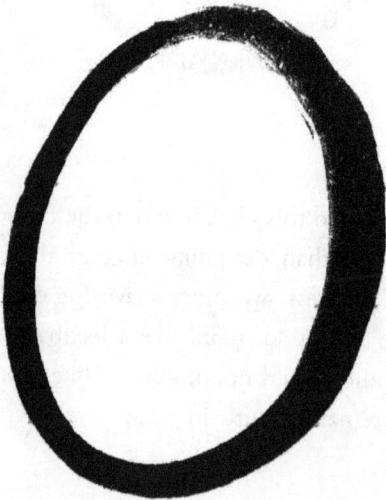

So what would be the effects of looking at products more holistically, and simplified? Well, we'd see an iPhone not just as something in our pocket, but also something in a landfill, and remove the third stage of Decay from something we externalize to others. Instead, we would view these things as responsibilities, changes we caused in the universe to satisfy ourselves, rather than "use" product with externalized, out of sight/mind decay stage.

How would this effect manufacturing? It would put greater emphasis on component reparability, durability, and overall environmental friendliness of manufacturing pieces. This is in stark contrast to the planned obsolescence and unplanned, but price oriented production of cheap, built to price with lowered life spec goods we currently encounter, sadly, at a time when we could make things that last longer than ever before.

TLDR; Decay is part of a product, not something that happens when you are done with it. Products are responsibilities to those whom cause them to be built. We need a new language and mindset to keep up with the reality that decay is not an externalized stage, but one the producer and product buyer are inherently responsible for causing, and dealing with.

MEANING

We make beautiful images.

We share them.

People 'like' them

People 'share' them

Why?

A story is being told.

And people are narrating a part of their life with these images.

For many years, folks have turned to the arts to narrate their stories. For the emotions, it may have been a painting, a poem, or a song. And for experience, perhaps a movie. No single medium has conquered a range of sense, but all have been used to by a viewer to complete a piece of a puzzle; the puzzle of what they are feeling.

The arts can be cathartic for the artist. But they can also be cathartic for the audience. And they can narrate the audience's life.

So what is it all for?

Essentially, to help show meaning.

Art can highlight, solidify, extract and contain meaning as people view art and assign art relevance.

It becomes a useful art the second a person views it.

Without the human viewing and assigning it, the image is meaningless.

So what does it say about a society that spends most of

its time trading art?
I think it says we are searching for narration, and at a deeper level, relevance, and meaning.

CARS AND UNNECCESARY COMPLICATION

Dec 21 2013

There are many things I don't like, that I make compromises on to live in the world today:
    Cars
    Phones
    Social media
    Promotional website for various businesses I run
    Business cards

A lot of the reason I don't like these things, is they take time out of your life, for maintaining the thing.

Facebook is a good example. I like being able to talk to friends every now and again, don't like having to wade through a huge amount of stuff to do it.

Phones: I like being able to find my spouse when we get lost from each other in a store, don't like getting calls or texts though.

Promotional websites: I like being able to refer to a thing I'm doing by directing someone to something at a fixed URL, don't like having to figure a way to display it, because, well, web design is horribly dated and tacky compared to any other medium, save for glossy DJ fliers: those are just as bad.

With cars, I don't like owning something I cannot fix, and that if I can fix, it costs lots of money to fix. I also don't like owning something that is over complicated that, while I can fix, I now need to fix, because it's breaking. Especially when that breakage doesn't bother me, but will bother a state inspection. Like power windows. Fuck power windows. I'd rather just have a manual crank and not spend my Saturday in a hot junkyard pulling a window motor out of a dead version of my car.

If I could figure out a way to make it work, I would opt for the following:

Walking instead of car

A Way to communicate with friends that was easy for them to communicate with me that   didn't require its own separate apparatus like Facebook does

A phone that could only text and receive text from spouse and doctors

Magically be able to reference product or service I have without a website

But, well, walking isn't really practical in the city I live, scooter, as fun as they are, won't work with a baby or a spouse, riding in rain on scooter sucks, and riding in winter on scooter sucks too.

So I have a car. Rather, we have this car. And we are thankful to have it. It got us through a couple summers with its cold A/C, and took us many places we wouldn't have been able to see. And it's pretty nice, one of the nicest I've ever owned. And when money got tight, I was able to sell my older, higher mileage car, and cut expenses to rely on this one. Also, it was given to us by family, so it was generally a win-win situation.

But like all machines, they break down. We knew when getting it, that it had transmission issues. But the issues never really developed to be a problem, until earlier this year. As this car had working A/C, and was in good condition otherwise, we decided to rebuild the transmission. Everything else seemed fine, so it seemed like a good idea. But a few months after rebuilding the transmission this year for $1700 then doing the normal brake changes, the car decided to blow a hole through one of its valves. (Note: 1998 was a horrible year for Honda Accord automatic transmissions, and third gear likes to grind out then sprinkle itself all over the other gears like some kind of pixie dust of death.)

The problem revealed itself to us in the mountains of West Virginia. The car began to sound a bit like a helicopter. After confirming that it wasn't just my ears and altitude playing tricks on me, we Slowed down to a rest stop, at which we realized the idle was really, really messed up. I popped the hood: nothing loose. Shit. Hoping it was the altitude we were at, and possibly the ECU was having issues adjusting fuel flow based on the changes, we drove on home.

The next day I conclude cylinder 4 isn't firing. Swap plugs and wires, still not firing. So I called up a buddy who had a compression gauge. Run the test, nothing. Nothing at all. We swap out to a different cylinder, just to make sure we have enough power to crank; yeah, cylinder 3 works. But cylinder 4 is dead. Buddy also had an OBDII scanner, so we pop that in, and it looks like the distributor is going to fail as well pretty soon. Not fun stuff.

As fixing the valve problems is a rather complicated process to by oneself, and expensive to have done by a shop, the options are: a) Swap in a different engine, or b) get a different car. So, it looks like the spouse and I are buying a car in January.

Don't get me wrong, I do enjoy working on some things: Trying to get a stubborn race car started with my dad is fun. But trying to fix a modern car is kind of like climbing a small mountain just to eat a bowl of instant mashed potatoes: Difficult. And though you're thankful for the sustenance, the reward is bland and overshadowed by the amount of seemingly unnecessary, overcomplicated work involved. And that thing, passion, that can be summoned up to help one overcome such things in the pursuit of a goal, isn't evoked at all.

And that is just one of the problems with modern cars. They are also not designed to be worked on by anyone but a specialist. They use almost exactly the same technology as they did in 1910, yet they've overcomplicated them to the point where figuring out what is actually going on requires a computer, an expensive computer. A computer that is more technologically advanced than the one a space shuttle uses to calculate trajectories. And that, to control and command a relatively simple combustion engine, is ridiculous.

I suppose it also stings a bit, because I realize, a lot of the complication comes from the desire of companies to build something new; a new model, not necessarily better, but different, with new parts, meaning that a part from this year won't fit on this other year, not because it's better, but because of redesigning the part for reasons that have little to do with functionality and much to do with style and fashion.

The bottom line: folks with little money like me don't need to be buying cars that were designed for fashion and style. We need standardized workhorse, utilitarian, vehicles. Things that have a large parts supply, can easily be swapped out, diagnosed, and are designed with use in mind.

Now, such vehicles do exist, they care called used police cars. But they get 15 mpg.

I am really not looking forward to buying a different car, as once you realize the design issues inherently involved, you realize you're just buying another shade of the same thing. But there are some smarter choices I can make: Run from automatic transmissions. Look for those window cranks. And buy the vehicle expecting that this situation may repeat itself, so get something that is worth saving.

I'm hoping for the best.

ON LES PAULS AND DECISION MAKING

Dec 21 2013

A friend of mine asked me to help her find a good Les Paul guitar recently. It was to be a gift for her boyfriend, and as he was an experienced player, it had to be a good one. It was also something of a replacement. Apparently, he had an extremely nice version of one years ago, and so the goal was to try and get something that would be like that one. Maybe better. Sounding like a fun adventure, I agreed, and we began scouring the internet to look for a guitar.

Now, guitars are very temperamental instruments. It's not just the woods used, or the parts, but how it all comes together. How they complement each other. On paper, almost every guitar is great. But in a guitar playing reality, many are not. So setting out to find a good one requires one of two things a) luck, or b) playing a bunch to find one.

If we were shooting blind, with no guitar to compare to, this would have been an easy task. But as we had a model name, a picture, a color, and stories of how awesome this old guitar was, we had a lot to stack up against.

Les Pauls are funny instruments. First, they are heavy. Heavier than your typical Stratocaster. But the secret to a good guitar, is less moisture in the wood. Moisture equals a dead sound. Less moisture means more acoustic resonance. Less moisture also means a lighter guitar. If you have two identical models of the same guitar and one is lighter, the lighter one almost always sounds better. If it doesn't, there is probably some other issue at hand.

But Gibson, the manufacturer of the Les Paul, has done some odd things to Les Pauls over the years, namely, in using different techniques to make them lighter, other than reducing moisture content. For some models and years, they simply drilled holes in the body. You can't see this, as a Les Paul has at least two parts of wood to the body, one being the actual body wood, and the other, a thin piece of carved wood that you see as its top. For other years and models, they skeletonized the body, 'chambering' it, so that all that is left of the thickest part of the body is almost just its edges. This results in a resonant guitar, but not with the same amount of sustain, as a solid body guitar. It can also result in an odd sounding feedback, compared to a more solid version. And then there are the woods, different types of body wood has been used to reduce weight, or different tops, and then, due to problems obtaining the typical fret board woods, different choices there as well. All of which effect sustain, weight, resonance, playability, and the overall value of the guitar down the line.

Beginning our quest, we were able to find a good looking one locally, so I went by to play it. While it was not a bad Les Paul, it was not a good one. And for $1400, you don't really want a passable one.

Option two arrived in the form of one found online. It looked good, but we couldn't play it as it was 1000 miles from us. So we took a risk and told the salesman the situation, and asked if he, as an experienced guitar player would play it, and tell us if it's one of the better ones he has. Putting trust into a person trying to sell an instrument probably depends just as much on the ethics of the person you are trusting as much as the amount of other guitars he has available. He came back to us and said the guitar was nothing to write home about, but he did have one that was very good, around the same price, but the color wasn't what we were really looking for. And comparably, the price for the model was a little high.

Fortunately, my friend's diligent searching of web stock found us another local one to check out. The color was good, the price was good, and it was from a local dealer that, if her boyfriend didn't like the guitar, they would take it back. So we went in to play it. Within a few seconds, it was apparent this was a good guitar. Broken in nicely and easy to play, good sustain to the notes. I plugged it into an amp, sounded great.

So I went picking through the rest of the stock the store had, found a few marginal ones, and one very good one. Brought it over, it's a bit more in price than the one we came in for. I began comparing the two. And here you have the classic debacle of quality instruments. One has great quality, and an acceptable price. The other has a teensy more versatility, and a much higher price. And then you realize that, you have fucked yourself, just a little, by seeing the 1% better one. Any guitar player would love either of these, both are excellent, but you know one is a little bit better. And so you start to try and break down the price difference, and... Well just stop because the price difference is ridiculous. And so you put rationale in front of some other kind of rationale, and realize yes, this one you came for is the one that you will get because it's awesome, and yes there are better ones in the world but it's not worth it.

Probably the funniest thing about guitars, is out of years of playing different ones; great guitars, bad guitars... that by percentage, how many supposedly great models are marginal in quality. And accordingly, how much great music has probably been made on marginal examples of those instruments.

It's a weird process that occurs when we begin to research something we want to buy. I've heard a theory that our evolved sense of what was food acquisition; IE hunting, takes over when we search for something. And when we learn something is better, we hone in on it. Perhaps there is a bit of insecurity as well that comes in to play; as money is wages, and wages are our times, and we want to be valuable, and if we cannot get more money per hour, than at least we can maximize what we get for the money, so we look for deals, educate ourselves, to give a hunting advantage.

And being in this process, I find myself learning more about Les Pauls than I ever wanted to know. As a guitar player, I play to make songs. Songs about the problems in the world. Songs about love. Songs about wishing for more good things for those around me than what a lot of people are willing to allow themselves. In the absolute sense, cut and dry, I don't give a shit if my guitar was made in 1970 or 1991, or if it was made when they were bought by a huge company or at the old factory they originated in.

And coming to that conclusion has political ramifications, because as an artist I want to shut down the rational and spec-sheet reading part of myself, just get a tool and get the song down, but maybe I know that one company pays a living wage to its employees and the cheaper guitar comes from a factory that might dump it's waste into a river, in a community that doesn't have the money to clean it up, because the company was given a tax break as incentive to move there, and so no real income is showing up yet to offset the true cost of their operation on the land around it. And to fuck that up, that even as bad as that is, that the job around all those chemicals may be the only choice those folks have for work right now.

GREY. AREA.

I wish I didn't have to make any of these choices. I wish suitable tools would just appear when needed, disappear when not, and that be that. And its sounds like an amazing dream. Until I realize that the context in which these things are built in is what I really want to have no part of. The weather was colder, so maybe the wood didn't dry out. Or sales were down, so the wood got to sit longer. Or the neck has a different wood because the rainforests are getting depleted and they had to figure a way not to fuck the earth up, or go to jail, yet still somehow, produce guitars.

And then I ask myself; why should it be easy to decide?

That tree took effort to grow, the workers took effort to go to work, the company took effort to get it here, the sales team took effort to try and sell it, it took effort to obtain the money, so why shouldn't a similar amount of effort go into deciding which process to support, and ultimately, which guitar to make these songs on?

Contemplating these situations, I realize it is precisely because I care about these things that the decision becomes hard.

Whenever I get bogged down in specs and comparisons, I am reminded of when I bought an acoustic. I had gone to my favorite shop in town, as I knew they only kept the good ones on the walls. After playing for an hour, I was at an impasse, two sounded really well, but not great

The shop owner came in, and offered to restring another guitar, just to try and see if something else might move the decision along. At the very moment he finished his sentence, the high 'E' string snapped right off a Martin acoustic on the wall in front of us. Stunned, and somewhat amazed, as I had been in this room for an hour and no one had touched that guitar, I said 'Let's try that one'. And it was perfect. Amazing. And went on to be the guitar I recorded a few EPs on.

Sometimes, it's important to just allow yourself to be open to what is in front of you, rather than forcing something to happen. And that means leaving empty handed more than not. But it also means gathering a deeper respect for your values, and yourself for respecting them.

In the end, my friend bought the Les Paul we went in for, and her boyfriend absolutely loved it. I am happy I could help her find a good one.

ON EMPATHY

Life is a quirk of the universe. A quirk that happens to build up from the very thing that created it, whatever you believe that to be.

But one thing is for sure, life is a precious thing.

When we begin to examine all of the atrocities of the world, we can see the world as a cold, unfair place. And that may be true to some extent. But it's important in seeing such atrocity, to remember why it's so sad: Because life is a precious thing.

We don't cry for others because of their lack of suffering. We cry because of the suffering. And we cry because the thought of someone's life being taken up with suffering, is the waste of a precious thing.

Do you see the theme here?

It is precisely because of the amazingness of life, the scarcity of life, that the atrocities of the world hurt so badly.

So in seeing these atrocities; poverty, famine, war, and so many other conditions and acts and conditions that bring suffering to humanity, it is important to not forget that it is precisely the beauty of life and the living, that it seems so bad.

Else, we focus solely on the conditions, and forget why we care.

And this last bit, that human beings themselves are hardwired to have empathy with one another, is the brightest hope in it all. Many problems have been solved by appealing to another's sense of empathy.

A bit of a mindfuck, but it rings true to me.

www.ingramcontent.com/pod-product-compliance
Lightning Source LLC
Chambersburg PA
CBHW021828020426
42334CB00014B/533